Time *for* Reading Comprehension

T0363264

3

Tess Finneran

HUNTER
EDUCATION
NIGHTINGALE

Copyright © 2014 Tess Finneran
Time for Reading Comprehension Book 3

Published by:
Hunter Education Nightingale
ABN: 69 055 798 626
PO Box 547
Warners Bay NSW 2282
Ph: 0417 658 777
email: sales@huntereducation.com.au
website: www.huntereducationnightingale.com.au

Cover Design: Brooke Lewis

National Library of Australia Card No.
and ISBN 978 - 1 - 922242 - 18 - 1

Time for Reading Comprehension
Book 3

About this Book

Time for Reading Comprehension Book 3 is one of a series designed to develop confidence in reading and competence in all areas of language. Units have been developed around the objectives of the new Australian Curriculum and K-10 syllabus guidelines. Specific attention has been given to a wide variety of text types along with the development of understanding, interpreting and responding when reading.

The book contains 29 units each addressing a different text type. The topics introduced encourage talking, listening and writing about the stories presented. Activities are developed under the headings of understanding, interpreting and responding. By addressing activities under these headings, the specific reading skill is practised and reinforced.

The 29 units provided in this book give the teacher the freedom to cater to the individual child, a small group or a class as a whole. Specific aspects of reading can be identified, practised and developed within the context of each unit as the year progresses. It is suggested that the child moves at his or her own pace and level of ability with this book. However, a teacher can select specific components within each text type to help the child master a particular aspect of reading. It is essential to keep a record of reading skills so that the teacher can provide practice activities that have been identified as a weakness by a child's past performance.

While the activities develop skills over time the objectives set out in the curriculum will be addressed with the introduction of more advanced reading skills as the year progresses when working with this book.

A full set of answers is provided at the back of this book for the busy teacher and parent who has a child that can work independently in reading. The child should be encouraged to read and given appropriate rewards and awards when he or she attains success in developing the skills associated with that of a good reader.

Message to Parents

Time for Reading Comprehension Book 3 will help parents understand grammar, punctuation, spelling and writing. Use that understanding to help your child develop the skills to be confident in all aspects of Reading. Encourage, praise and help where you can at home. Your encouragement will play a big part in your child's learning at school and beyond.

This is a legend from Africa. Legends often try to explain how something came to be.

Once, when the world was young, the crocodile had smooth, golden skin. Crocodile spent all his day when the sun was hot in the muddy waters of the river and only came out onto the land at night. Because of this, his skin stayed beautifully soft and smooth. All the other animals admired Crocodile's skin and often told him so.

Crocodile loved to hear what the animals said about his skin and so, he started to come out of the water when the sun was shining. He just wanted to hear them say over and over how lovely he was. But, in time, he became very proud and he began to think that he was much better than the other animals. His sweet nature changed and he started bossing the animals around. They were upset by this and so started to keep away from Crocodile. Very few animals now said how lovely he was, but Crocodile spent all day on the river bank, in the hot sun, hoping for nice words.

All of the days that Crocodile was spending in the sun were changing his skin. It became thicker and bumpier and uglier every day. It was not smooth and golden now. One day, Crocodile looked at himself and knew that he was lovely no longer. He slipped into the river. Even today, Crocodile will hide under the water when he hears people coming, just leaving his eyes and his nose above the surface.

Understanding

1. Colour the bubble which best fits each sentence.

a. At first, Crocodile's skin was
- ◯ soft and yellow
- ◯ thick and golden
- ◯ gold-coloured, but bumpy

b. The river water was
- ◯ clear
- ◯ warm
- ◯ muddy

c. In the beginning, Crocodile spent all his day
- ◯ in the muddy river
- ◯ laying in the warm sun
- ◯ on the bank of the river

d. At first, Crocodile's nature was
- ◯ proud
- ◯ gentle
- ◯ bossy

e. After a time, Crocodile began to spend time on the bank
- ◯ all day long
- ◯ in the evening
- ◯ in the afternoon

f. Crocodile began to think
- ◯ his skin was just as lovely as before
- ◯ he was better than the other animals
- ◯ the other animals were jealous of hir

g. Finally, Crocodile's skin was
- ◯ a little different
- ◯ much smoother
- ◯ completely changed

. Colour the bubble that best fits each question or sentence.

a. 'Once when the world was young...'
This tells us
- ⬭ the story is a legend
- ⬭ the story is based on history
- ⬭ the story is for young people

b. The change in the crocodile's nature
was caused by
- ⬭ pride
- ⬭ worry
- ⬭ unhappiness

c. The other animals were upset by
- ⬭ the crocodile's changed skin
- ⬭ the crocodile's changed habits
- ⬭ the crocodile's changed nature

d. The legend suggests that
- ⬭ the crocodile still has a sweet nature
- ⬭ the crocodile was punished for his pride
- ⬭ the other animals were jealous of the crocodile

e. The end of the text tells us that
- ⬭ the crocodile is shy about the way he looks now
- ⬭ the crocodile looks much the same as he always did
- ⬭ the crocodile still thinks he's better than the other animals

Responding

. Answer the questions in full sentences.

a. Imagine you are one of the animals. Write what you would say to the crocodile-

- When he was beautiful: _____

_____

- When he started to be bossy: _____

_____

- After his skin changed: _____

_____

b. Was it fair that Crocodile became ugly? Give reasons. _____

_____

_____

c. What lesson for us does the story have?_____

_____

_____

Soil is the top layer of the Earth's crust. It is made up of water, air, tiny pieces of rock, minerals and bits of living and dead plants and animals. Without soil, nothing could grow on Earth. Soil takes a long time to form. To make just two centimetres of top soil takes 500 years, so we need to care for our soil.

There are three main kinds of soil. These are sand, clay and silt. Some soils are a mixture of all of these kinds. Different places on Earth have different types of soil. Farmers grow different sorts of crops in different sorts of soil.

Soil usually has three layers: top soil, subsoil and bedrock. Top soil has all the **nutrients** that help plants grow well. It is never more than 30 centimetres deep. The subsoil is not as rich as top soil, but some plants put down deep roots into it. The bottom layer is bedrock which i made up of broken rocks and soil.

Earthworms, which live in the top layer of soil, chew up bits of plants and give out waste whic makes the soil richer. Mice and moles make burrows through it and this helps to **aerate** it. This means to bring air into the soil.

Soil can be many colours. Yellow or red soil shows that there is iron in it. Dark brown or blac soil means it has a lot of animal or plant pieces that have rotted in it. Wet soil is darker than dry soil.

Good top soil can be lost. When this happens, the soil left is not good for growing crops. Heavy rain can wash away the top soil or it can be blown away by strong wind. This happens if the soil does not have any plants growing on it, and is bare.

Understanding

1. Answer these questions in full sentences.

a. What are the three main types of soil? _____

_____

b. What are the three layers of soil? _____

_____

c. Which is the richest layer? _____

d. Which layer do earthworms live in? _____

e. How do mice make soil better? _____

_____

Circle the correct word in each set of brackets.

a. It takes (200 / 500) years for two centimetres of top soil to form.

b. Top soil is never more than 30 (mm / cm) deep.

c. The second layer of soil is called (bedrock / subsoil).

d. Soil can be carried away by (birds / wind).

e. Earthworms chew up bits of (dirt / plants).

Interpreting

Colour the bubble which best fits each question or sentence.

a. The text suggests that top soil is
- ⬭ full of rocks
- ⬭ very important
- ⬭ not as good as subsoil

b. Soil with iron in it can be
- ⬭ black
- ⬭ yellow
- ⬭ dark brown

c. The word in the text which means to bring air into soil is
- ⬭ aerate
- ⬭ burrow
- ⬭ nutrient

d. What makes plants grow well?
- ⬭ iron
- ⬭ nutrients
- ⬭ deep roots

e. Why is it a big problem if top soil is lost?
- ⬭ Only the rocks will be left.
- ⬭ The wind may blow the soil away.
- ⬭ It will be impossible to grow plants.

f. Which of these statements is true?
- ⬭ We can make new top soil.
- ⬭ There is hardly any top soil left.
- ⬭ Different crops need different kinds of soil.

g. What conclusion can be drawn from the last paragraph?
- ⬭ Strong winds blow plants away.
- ⬭ Plants grow just as well in subsoil.
- ⬭ Plants help to stop soil from blowing away.

Responding

a. Write down two things from the text that you did not know before.

- _____

- _____

b. Find two synonyms for 'soil'. _____ _____

A Dreadful Day!

Dad's alarm didn't ring at all,
So the family woke up really late.
For breakfast I had to have Corn Pops,
The cereal I really hate.

I searched all over my room
Looking for my clean sports skirt,
In the end, I wore the other one,
Covered with grass stains and dirt.

We ran all the way to the bus stop,
But the school bus didn't wait.
We walked a long way to school,
So, of course, we were quite late.

I really don't like doing Maths
And we did it all morning long.
I tried hard to do my best,
But I still had a lot of it wrong.

Things got worse and worse,
Throughout that dreadful day,
I'd forgotten to bring my hat to school,
So, at sport, I couldn't play.

At After-school Care, I fell over,
And whacked my chin and my knee,
I had to sit quietly till Mum came
And hugged and comforted me.

By Charlotte Grey

Understanding

1. Circle either T (true) or F (false) for each statement.

a. Mum's alarm did not ring.   T   F

b. Everyone woke up late.   T   F

c. The poet hates Corn Flakes.   T   F

d. The children were driven to school.   T   F

e. It was mufti day at school.   T   F

f. The poet likes Maths.   T   F

g. The poet didn't play sport.   T   F

h. The poet goes to After-school Care.   T   F

i. The poet forgot to bring a book to school.   T   F

. Write a full sentence to answer each question about the poem.

a. Who wrote the poem? _____

b. What two things does the poet not like?

_____

c. Why couldn't the poet take part in sport at school?

_____

d. Write the line that tells you the children's school is not near their house.

_____

e. Who picked the poet up at the end of the day?

_____

Interpreting

. Colour the bubble that best fits each question or sentence.

a. How many sports skirts does the girl have?
- ◯ one
- ◯ two
- ◯ we can't tell

b. Why did the children miss the bus?
- ◯ The bus left early.
- ◯ They ran all the way.
- ◯ They arrived at the stop too late.

c. The words that tell us the day didn't improve are
- ◯ couldn't play
- ◯ worse and worse
- ◯ whacked my chin

d. 'I don't really like doing Maths'... 'I tried hard to do my best' These lines show us that the poet
- ◯ sees no point in trying hard at Maths
- ◯ really hates having Maths all morning
- ◯ finds Maths difficult, but still makes an effort

e. The poem suggests that when her mum came, the girl felt
- ◯ better
- ◯ worse
- ◯ the same

Responding

. Write a response to each question in a full sentence.

a. Where do you think the grass stains on her skirt might have come from?

_____

b. Do you feel sorry for the girl in the poem? Why or why not?

_____

c. Have you ever had a day like this? Describe it.

_____

_____

How to Make Ladybirds

What you need –

- Some smooth round or oval-shaped rocks.

- Red or orange craft paint.

- Black craft paint.

- Wiggly craft eyes.

- A black permanent marker.

- Craft glue.

What you do –

- Scrub the rocks very well.

- Paint about one quarter of the rock black for the head. Let it completely dry.

- Paint the rest of the rock in red or orange. Let it dry.

- With the permanent marker, draw a line down the back of the ladybird.

- Paint dots with black craft paint.

- Attach the eyes with craft glue.

- When everything is completely dry, spray the ladybird with sealer spray.

Understanding

1. *Number the steps 1 to 5 to show the order needed to make a ladybird.*

a. ☐   Colour one quarter black.

b. ☐   Make dots with black paint.

c. ☐   Clean the rocks.

d. ☐   Glue the eyes on.

e. ☐   Paint all the rest orange.

Use either 'before' or 'after' to make these statements true.

a. Draw a line down the back of the ladybird _____ painting the dots.

b. Let the paint dry completely _____ you have painted the head.

c. Glue on the eyes _____ you spray with sealer spray.

d. _____ beginning to paint, scrub the rocks.

e. Paint the rock red or orange _____ you have painted the head.

f. Spray with sealer spray _____ you have completed the ladybird.

Interpreting

Colour the bubble which best fits each question or sentence.

a. The words under 'What you need' are written as
  ◯ a list
  ◯ a note
  ◯ sentences

b. Why must the ladybird be completely dry before spraying with sealer spray?
  ◯ The ladybird has to be finished.
  ◯ The colours might run if it isn't dry.
  ◯ You might want to change the colours.

c. Which of these tells you what to do?
  ◯ let it dry
  ◯ down the back
  ◯ with sealer spray

d. The craft glue is used to
  ◯ cover
  ◯ fasten
  ◯ blotch

e. Making the dots is the _____ step.
  ◯ fourth
  ◯ fifth
  ◯ sixth

f. The purpose of this text is
  ◯ to amuse
  ◯ to instruct
  ◯ to persuade

Responding

Write a response to each question in a full sentence.

a. What are some reasons that this would be a good craft to do?

_____

b. What could the ladybird be used for?

_____

Captain Tilly's Treasure

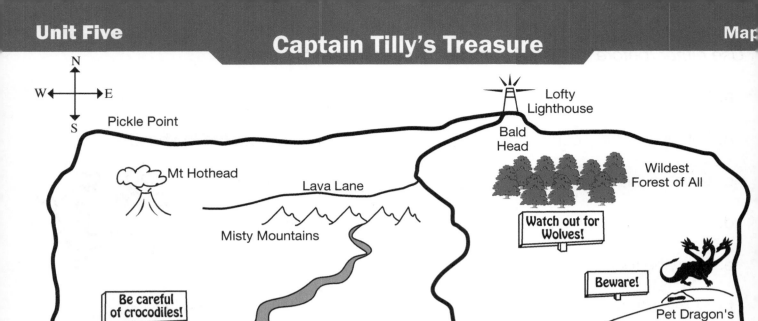

Understanding

1. Circle either T (true) or F (false) for each statement.

    a. There are three forests.   T   F

    b. The lighthouse is at Pickle Point.   T   F

    c. The village is near Bluefish Bay.   T   F

    d. There are wolves in the Wild Forest.   T   F

    e. The Red River begins in the Misty Mountains.   T   F

    f. The quicksand is in the Shady Swamps.   T   F

    g. Lava Lane goes to the Pet Dragon's Den.   T   F

    h. There are less than twenty houses in the village.   T   F

    i. Trickle Creek runs into Bluefish Bay.   T   F

    j. The sail-maker is next to the baker.   T   F

. *Write a full sentence to answer each question about the map.*

a. Explain how you would get from the village to Mt Hothead.

_____

_____

b. Imagine you are travelling north from Blunderbuss Bay to Pickle Point. Describe your journey.

_____

_____

c. How do you think Mt Hothead got its name? _____

_____

d. The map warns of a number of dangers. What are they? _____

_____

e. How far is it roughly from Bald Head to Blunderbuss Bay?

_____

f. Explain how each of the shops would be useful to pirates.

Sail-maker: _____

Sword-maker: _____

Boat-builder: _____

Baker:_____

Pirate Clothes Shop: _____

g. Which of these is not on the island?
○ Leafy Lane   ○ Wilder Forest   ○ Prickle Point   ○ Shady Swamps

h. Besides the shopkeepers, how do the other villagers make their living?

_____

_____

Responding

. *Captain Tilly wrote directions in code to help her friends find her treasure.*
Solve the code and mark where the treasure is hidden on the map.

a. eht erusaert si txen ot eht s'nogard ned - od eb luferac !

_____

b. Why do you think Captain Tilly hid it there?

_____

Olivia the Princess

Olivia was a princess in the faraway land of Happily-Ever-After. She was the only child of her parents, King Boris and Queen Charlotte, and so she had everything she could wish for. Her dresses of silver and gold cloth filled six wardrobes and she had fifty-seven pairs of shoes. Her toys filled three rooms.

If Olivia wanted a snack, her own chef would whip up some pancakes or pizza or popcorn. If she wanted to go out, she had a small coach pulled by four milk-white ponies to ride in and two nannies and a footman to go with her. She just had to say what she wished for and it was granted. Grand-mama, the old Queen Serena, thought Olivia was spoiled and told her that she needed to find something useful to do.

However, Olivia was bored! One day, she was in the castle library and she spied a book with the title, "Circus Tricks to Teach Your Unicorn". Now, Olivia had her own unicorn, along with three cats, four dogs, five rabbits, six talking parrots and a very fat white mouse. (Olivia loved pets!) She leafed through the book. How much fun it would be to teach her unicorn to count to five by tapping its hoof or even to jump through a hoop on fire! Her mind was made up. Yes, she would train her unicorn, whose name was Peppy, and everyone would be so surprised. Grand-mama would see that she had found something useful to do. Perhaps, Peppy and she would be able to join a circus and travel the world. That sounded a lot more exciting than being a princess!

Olivia was just leaving the library when she met her father, King Boris. "What do you have there?" he asked, seeing the large red-covered book.

"Um, um," said Olivia, putting the book behind her. "Isn't it a lovely day? I'm going to have a picnic with my dolls."

King Boris beamed at her. He'd forgotten about the book already. "Have a lovely time, darling," he said, fondly.

Olivia walked quietly down the hallway away from her father, but as soon as she turned the corner, she dashed out the door and headed towards the stables where Peppy was kept. She wanted to get started on teaching him straight away. She could already see herself as the star of the circus. "Peppy," she called, "we are going to have so much fun!"

Understanding

1. Use the narrative to answer these questions.

   a. How many wardrobes did Olivia have? _____

   b. Who was Olivia's mother? _____

   c. How many pets did Olivia have altogether? _____

   d. How many pairs of shoes did Olivia have? _____

   e. Where did Peppy live? _____

   f. Who told Olivia to 'find something useful to do'? _____

Colour the bubble that best fits each question or sentence.

a. Grand-mama's attitude towards Olivia is
- ◯ loving
- ◯ surprised
- ◯ uninterested
- ◯ disapproving

b. Why does Olivia say, "Um, um"?
- ◯ She thinks he is cranky.
- ◯ She doesn't want to tell him what the book is.
- ◯ She doesn't want to tell him where she's been.
- ◯ She is tired of being asked questions all the time.

c. She hides the book behind her back
- ◯ because it is his book
- ◯ because he will want to help
- ◯ because she wants to keep it a secret
- ◯ because she shouldn't take books from the library

d. Olivia dashes outside because she is
- ◯ spoilt
- ◯ bored
- ◯ excited
- ◯ frightened

e. Olivia is looking forward to
- ◯ surprising people
- ◯ possibly joining a circus
- ◯ having a more exciting life
- ◯ all of these

f. Another good title for this story would be
- ◯ "Olivia's Circus."
- ◯ "Olivia's Great Idea."
- ◯ "Peppy the Unicorn."
- ◯ "Olivia's Terrible Problem."

g. This story is
- ◯ a legend
- ◯ a recount
- ◯ a factual story
- ◯ a fantasy story

Write a response to each question in a full sentence.

a. Olivia doesn't tell her father the truth about what she is going to do. What do you think of her behaviour?

_____

_____

b. What do you think will happen in the story now? _____

_____

c. What is one way in which Olivia's life is different to yours? _____

_____

d. How do you know this is a fantasy story? _____

_____

The Woolly Mammoth

The Woolly Mammoth was a prehistoric animal which looked a little like a modern-day elephant. It became extinct 10 000 years ago, but frozen bodies of mammoths have been discovered so we know today what they looked like.

Size: Fully grown male mammoths could be more than three metres tall and could weigh up to six tons. Female mammoths were smaller than this. Mammoth calves usually weighed about 90 kg when they were born.

Appearance: Woolly Mammoths were covered all over with thick fur. This was because they lived in cold places in Europe and North America. The blonde, brown or black fur had two layers: long guard hairs on top and a coat of shorter fur underneath. The fur was very greasy and this kept out water. The grease helped the fur to stick together, too, and this kept body heat in and chilly air out. Unlike a modern elephant, the mammoth had very small ears. This was to stop heat being lost from the body.

The fearsome-looking mammoth had a high domed forehead, very big shoulders and a sloping back. The mammoth's huge curved tusks might weigh from 45 to 90 kg!

Food: Woolly Mammoths were **herbivorous**. This means they ate grass, parts of plants and mosses. Scientists think they may have eaten for up to twenty hours a day to get enough food to give their huge bodies energy.

Enemies: Woolly Mammoths, being so large, had few enemies. However, humans hunted them very successfully in packs. Although climate change played a part, hunting was the main reason that the numbers of Woolly Mammoths became fewer and fewer.

Understanding

1. Tick the bubble that has information from this text.

a. ⬭ Woolly mammoths lived in Europe.

b. ⬭ Frozen mammoth bodies have been found in Russia.

c. ⬭ Woolly Mammoths could have blonde fur.

d. ⬭ Dwarf mammoths survived until 4000 years ago.

e. ⬭ Male mammoths were bigger than female ones.

f. ⬭ Mammoths had thick fat under the fur.

g. ⬭ Woolly Mammoths sometimes ate moss.

h. ⬭ Woolly Mammoths roared loudly.

i. ⬭ Newborn Woolly Mammoth calves could weigh 90 kg.

j. ⬭ The mammoth's tusks were curved.

Complete these activities.

a. The Woolly Mammoth's outer fur is called _____.

b. Fully grown male Woolly Mammoths could weigh _____.

c. The Woolly Mammoth had a _____ forehead.

d. The mammoth's shoulders were _____ and its back was _____.

e. Woolly Mammoths were found in Europe and _____.

f. Woolly Mammoths may have eaten as long as_____ every day.

Interpreting

Colour the bubble that best fits each question or sentence.

a. Which statement best expresses the ideas in the first sentence?
- ◯ The Woolly Mammoth looked a lot like a modern elephant.
- ◯ The Woolly Mammoth looked exactly like a modern elephant.
- ◯ The Woolly Mammoth looked a little bit like a modern elephant.
- ◯ The Woolly Mammoth did not look anything like a modern elephant.

b. The text suggests that
- ◯ Mammoths had very little energy.
- ◯ Mammoths had quite a few enemies.
- ◯ Mammoths may have survived somewhere.
- ◯ Humans were the main danger to mammoths.

c. The text describes the Woolly Mammoth's appearance as
- ◯ extinct
- ◯ prehistoric
- ◯ herbivorous
- ◯ fearsome-looking

d. Which word in the last paragraph shows that a different idea has been introduced?
- ◯ reason
- ◯ enemies
- ◯ However
- ◯ successfully

e. Which book might this text be part of?
- ◯ "Hunting the Mammoth."
- ◯ "The Mammoth Book of Stories."
- ◯ "Fascinating Prehistoric Animals."
- ◯ "Max the Mammoth's Adventure."

f. Why does the writer mention the weight of the tusks?
- ◯ To provide some facts.
- ◯ To introduce new ideas.
- ◯ To help us picture the size of the tusks.
- ◯ To show that they would have given the mammoth a headache.

g. The purpose of the text is to
- ◯ inform
- ◯ amuse
- ◯ instruct
- ◯ persuade

Responding

Circle the adjectives which could be used to describe the Woolly Mammoth.

slim   tall   silly   giant   scared   terrifying   massive   teeny

enormous   furry   bald   hairy   heavy   skinny   funny   hungry

Good morning, Mrs Topp and fellow students,

I have been thinking a lot about what I would do if I were the principal of this school. I have decided that there is definitely not enough fun! We spend all day working much too hard. I would change a lot of things so that school was more exciting and interesting.

First of all, I would have shorter hours in the classroom and longer recess times and lunchtimes. This would mean that students had more time to play and be with their friends. I is just as important that students learn how get on with other people as it is to learn sums and spelling. Playing games is good for fitness, too.

Secondly, if I were the principal, I would ban all homework! Students do enough learning in class time. However, people who were naughty could get homework as punishment instead of getting detention.

Another exciting thing I would do, if I were principal, would be to have days when everyone just had fun and didn't have any classroom work at all. We might have days when students and teachers made and flew kites. On hot days, everyone could have water games all day long and keep very cool. On another special day, students could come as their favourite super-heroes. (The teachers could do this, too!)

Finally, if I were principal, I would make sure the excursions were more thrilling. We are tired of the same old excursions to the zoo or the museum! Instead, there could be days out at a theme park such as Wild Water World.   There could even be camping in the bush.

Now that you have heard my ideas, I'm sure you will agree that school would be much more fun and that everyone would really enjoy themselves!

Understanding

1. Summarise the changes the speaker would make.

(i) _____

(ii) _____

_____

(iii) _____

_____

(iv) _____

_____

Complete these sentences.

a. The speaker believes there should be shorter _____.

b. Fitness is improved by _____.

c. _____ should be banned.

d. On hot days, there could be _____.

e. Excursions could be to _____ or _____.

Interpreting

Colour the bubble that best fits each question or sentence.

a. Why are brackets used at the end of the fourth paragraph?
- ⬭ To explain the sentence before.
- ⬭ To explain what superheroes are.
- ⬭ To give examples of superheroes.
- ⬭ To add more information about the special day.

b. A similar word to 'thrilling' is
- ⬭ joyful
- ⬭ active
- ⬭ exciting
- ⬭ frightening

c. The speaker wants to
- ⬭ use homework as a reward
- ⬭ have homework done at school
- ⬭ use homework as a punishment
- ⬭ cut down the amount of homework

d. The purpose of the speech is to
- ⬭ inform
- ⬭ amuse
- ⬭ explain
- ⬭ persuade

Responding

Write a response to each question in a full sentence.

a. Do you think these changes would be good? Give your reasons.

_____

_____

b. Are there any of these changes would you like to see in your school? Why?

_____

c. If you were principal, what are three changes you would make?

- _____
- _____
- _____

Riley's Diary

Monday, 3rd July

I can't wait for tomorrow! We are all going by the Moonshuttle to the Moon! Dad has work there until October. He is helping them set up a new hospital. I bet I won't sleep tonight!

Tuesday, 4th July

At last, we're on the rocket ship! We have special seats that will become beds tonight. The Moonshuttle was so noisy when we took off that we all had earmuffs to cut out a lot of the sound. It felt just as if a giant hand was pressing us down in our seats. The shuttle is quite small as it only takes 100 people. Mum said that some of the other rocket ships can carry up to 500 people.

Wednesday, 5th July

One day of our journey has gone and there are two more to go. Last night the steward folded out our seats into beds. She helped us get into our sleeping bags. They are fastened to the beds so we don't float away. I am going to watch "Space Kids" now on my iPop. Rosie has been playing with her dolls. Mum only let her bring three. She wanted to bring seven!

Thursday, 6th July

I wonder what living on the Moon will be like? Dad showed us some pictures. All the people live in little cabins under a big dome. The school is under a smaller dome, and the hospital will have its own dome, too. There is air to breathe in the domes. When we are at home or school, we can wear ordinary clothes, but when we go out of the domes we have to put on special suits with tanks of air on the backs. That will be strange. I'm going to play Chess with Rosie, now. She's pretty good for a six-year-old.

Friday, 7th July

Tonight we will arrive on the Moon! I am glad because it is getting a bit boring. Rosie is a bit sad because she is missing Tyson, our cat. I told her Nanna will look after him and give him lots of treats. Dad said that they have some cool sports on the Moon. When you do high jumps, you can jump five metres into the air and you land really gently because the gravity is less than on Earth! Dad said we will be able to go on some short trips at the weekends. We can travel on a Moon buggy that can go in rough places. We might even have a picnic. I wonder if aliens are true? That worries me a bit.

Understanding

1. Write a full sentence to answer each question about Riley's Diary.

    a. How did Riley spend his time on the trip?

_____

    b. How did Rosie spend her time?

_____

    c. What transport will the family use on the Moon?

_____

Circle T (true) or F (false) for each sentence.

a. Rosie brought seven dolls.   T   F

b. Riley watched "Spice Kids".   T   F

c. Wednesday was the second day of the trip.   T   F

d. Mum helped the children to get into their sleeping bags.   T   F

e. Dad said they will go camping on the Moon.   T   F

f. People have to wear special clothes under the domes.   T   F

g. The Moonshuttle carries 100 people.   T   F

h. Rosie left her dolls at Nanna's.   T   F

i. It is possible to jump five metres high on the Moon.   T   F

j. The family will stay on the Moon for about three months.   T   F

k. They will need earmuffs to go outside.   T   F

Interpreting

Colour the bubble that best fits each sentence.

a. Before the family can go from one dome to another, they have to
- ⬭ take a shuttle
- ⬭ get a Moon buggy
- ⬭ put on ordinary clothes
- ⬭ change into other clothes

b. When Riley says Rosie is 'pretty good' at chess he means
- ⬭ better than he is
- ⬭ not very good at all
- ⬭ quite skilled for her age
- ⬭ at least as good as he is

c. There are cool sports on the Moon. In the sentence 'cool' means
- ⬭ tiring
- ⬭ chilly
- ⬭ difficult
- ⬭ out of the ordinary

d. The text shows that Riley's attitude to his sister is
- ⬭ kind
- ⬭ happy
- ⬭ worried

e. Riley said 'as if a giant hand was pressing us down'
- ⬭ to show how take-off felt
- ⬭ to show why he covered his ears
- ⬭ to show how noisy it was
- ⬭ to show how slowly the rocket went

Responding

Answer each question in a complete sentence.

a. What do you think will be good about Riley's time on the Moon? _____

_____

b. What could be problems that Riley might have? _____

_____

c. Would you like to live on the Moon? Give your reasons. _____

_____

What Are Hailstones?

Every year there are many severe thunderstorms all over Australia and during them, hailstones may fall. These hailstones can cause great damage to buildings, cars and farmers' crops. What are hailstones and how do they form?

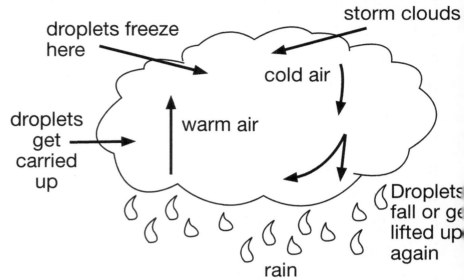

When there is a thunderstorm, the air inside it moves about. Warm air moves upwards and cold air moves downwards. Drops of water can be lifted up on warm air. As the droplets go up, the air becomes colder and they start to freeze. They begin to fall towards earth again with the downwards moving cold air.

The water droplets may thaw and fall to the ground as rain or they may be lifted up by more rising warm air. If that happens, they will freeze again, adding another layer of ice and getting bigger and bigger. Finally, the droplets are too heavy to be carried up and they fall to earth – as hail or rain.

Most hailstones are small – about the size of a pea, but huge hailstones as large as oranges or even grapefruit have fallen. When hailstones become very large they can be dangerous. If you were hit on the head by a huge hailstone, you would be seriously injured or even killed. The outside of cars can be dented and the windscreens and windows smashed by big hailstones. Tiles on the roofs of buildings can be smashed. Crops in the field can be completely destroyed.

Very bad thunderstorms in which hailstones fall can be a warning of even worse weather coming. Tornadoes can follow these storms.

Understanding

1. Tick the bubble that has information from this text.

   a. ⬭ Many thunderstorms occur every year all over Australia.

   b. ⬭ Drops are carried upwards on warm air.

   c. ⬭ Dark clouds tell us a storm is coming.

   d. ⬭ Most hailstones are quite small.

   e. ⬭ Hail causes millions of dollars' worth of damage every year.

   f. ⬭ Cars can have their glass smashed by hailstones.

   g. ⬭ Hailstones can look just like snow on the ground.

   h. ⬭ Tornadoes may follow severe thunderstorms.

Circle the correct word in each set of brackets.

a. Warm air moves (up / down) and cold air moves (up / down).

b. If frozen droplets thaw and freeze again they may become (rain / hail).

c. Each time a droplet is carried up, its size (increases /decreases).

d. When hailstones are too (heavy / frosty) they fall to earth.

e. Hailstones (sometimes / always) cause great damage.

f. Very bad thunderstorms may warn of (hailstones / tornadoes).

Interpreting

Colour the bubble that best fits each question or sentence.

a. 'If that happens, they will freeze again...' What does that stand for?
- ⬭ thawing
- ⬭ freezing
- ⬭ adding ice
- ⬭ being lifted

b. Why might hailstones be more dangerous as they increase in size?
- ⬭ They become larger.
- ⬭ They become colder.
- ⬭ There are more of them.
- ⬭ They hit things with more force.

c. A question has been used as a title
- ⬭ to express an opinion
- ⬭ because the writer doesn't know
- ⬭ to encourage the reader to find the answer
- ⬭ to encourage the reader to think about the question

d. The word which is closest in meaning to 'severe' is
- ⬭ long
- ⬭ noisy
- ⬭ terrible
- ⬭ sudden

e. The purpose of the diagram is
- ⬭ to add different information.
- ⬭ to show how hailstones form
- ⬭ to help you understand the text
- ⬭ to show the different types of air

f. The main idea of the fourth paragraph is
- ⬭ the effects of large hailstones
- ⬭ the movement of air in a storm
- ⬭ how dangerous thunderstorms are
- ⬭ how frequently hailstones cause damage

g. 'The frozen droplet' is an example of
- ⬭ an idea
- ⬭ a sentence
- ⬭ a description
- ⬭ technical language

h. The text might form part of which book?
- ⬭ "Wild Weather."
- ⬭ "The Biggest Hailstorm."
- ⬭ "Haunted Hailstone House."
- ⬭ "Harry Hailstone's Adventure."

Responding

'Frozen droplets' is an example of technical language.
Find three more examples of technical language in the text.

- _____

- _____

- _____

The Pied Piper
Part One

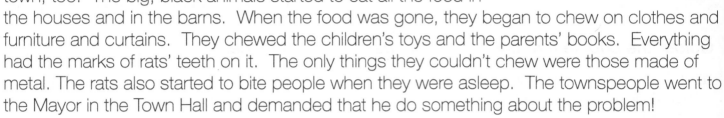

The Pied Piper is a very old legend. It has been told and retold many times. It has been written as a story by the Brothers Grimm and as a long poem by Robert Browning.

Once upon a time, there was a town in Germany called Hamelin. It was a very pleasant town and the townspeople liked living there very much. But, one day, something dreadful began to happen.

A great many rats suddenly began to make their homes in the town, too. The big, black animals started to eat all the food in the houses and in the barns. When the food was gone, they began to chew on clothes and furniture and curtains. They chewed the children's toys and the parents' books. Everything had the marks of rats' teeth on it. The only things they couldn't chew were those made of metal. The rats also started to bite people when they were asleep. The townspeople went to the Mayor in the Town Hall and demanded that he do something about the problem!

"What can I do?" he said, sighing noisily. "The dogs and cats are scared of the rats and have all run away." At that moment, they heard the notes of a flute, followed by a knock at the doo The door was opened to reveal a thin, fair man, dressed in bright red and yellow clothes.

"I will solve your problem," he said. "Pay me one thousand pieces of silver and I will take awa every rat. I am called the Pied Piper and I have helped other towns get rid of rats and toads and beetles."

"Yes," cried the delighted Mayor. "If you rid us of the rats, we will give you fifty times that much!" The townspeople all nodded in agreement.

So, the Pied Piper went out into the streets and played his flute. Squeaking and scurrying, the rats came from everywhere. They tumbled out of doorways and windows and drains and followed the sound of the flute. On through the town the strange piper marched until he came to the river. He didn't stop for a second, but walked right into the water. The rats all followed him and were swept away. Not a single rat could be seen! The townspeople and the Mayor cheered loudly.

Understanding

1. Tick T (true) or f (false) for each sentence.

    a. Hamelin was in Germany.   T   F

    b. Hamelin was near a river.   T   F

    c. The rats chewed tables, chairs and beds.   T   F

    d. The rats chewed metal cooking pots.   T   F

    e. There were no cats left in the town.   T   F

    f. The man wore orange and yellow clothes.   T   F

    g. The mayor offered one thousand pieces of silver.   T   F

Match the beginning of each sentence with its correct ending.
There are two more than you need.

| a danger to people | having rats all through their houses | stop at the river |

| tall and dark and dressed in red | tall and thin and brightly clothed |

| living in the pleasant town of Hamelin | one thousand pieces of silver |

| all of a sudden |

a. The townspeople enjoyed _____.

b. A large number of rats appeared _____.

c. The rats were _____.

d. The Piper was _____.

e. The Piper asked for _____.

f. The Piper did not _____.

Interpreting

Shade the bubble that best fits each question or sentence.

a. What is the purpose of the information given before the story?
- ◯ To show that the story is true.
- ◯ To tell where the story was set.
- ◯ To encourage you to read the poem.
- ◯ To show that this is a famous legend.

b. Which word tells you that the people wanted the Mayor to solve the problem?
- ◯ noisily
- ◯ problem
- ◯ something
- ◯ demanded

c. Why did the Mayor sigh?
- ◯ He was tired of the rats too.
- ◯ He was angry with the people.
- ◯ He was too busy to do anything.
- ◯ He didn't know what he could do.

d. A lot of detail is given about what the rats did
- ◯ to amuse the reader
- ◯ to bring in other ideas
- ◯ to help the reader picture the scene
- ◯ to make the reader sorry for the hungry rats

e. This text could form part of
- ◯ a poetry book
- ◯ a history book
- ◯ a book about rats
- ◯ a book of legends

Responding

Answer in complete sentences.

a. How would the townspeople have felt when the rats disappeared? _____

_____

b. What do you think will happen now? _____

_____

In the 1950's

When your grandparents were children in the 50's, life was very different to modern life. There were no dishwashers, microwaves or laptop computers. People worked and played in quite different ways to today.

Children usually walked to school or rode their bicycles, sometimes for long distances. An after-school snack was often homemade biscuits, not something popped in the microwave. If the weather was cold, the house would be heated with a wood or coal-burning fire, not with air-conditioning.

These days, it is not safe to play on the road because there is so much traffic. In the 1950's, the roads were not so busy and children often played hopscotch, football, skipping or chasin[g] games in the street.

Families generally ate their evening meals together. Meals were plain – stews or grilled meat and vegetables. No-one had heard of pizza yet! Sunday dinner was the most important meal of the week and it was always a roast – chicken or lamb. Afterwards, the dishes were washed by hand, not put into the dishwasher.

When the children had finished their homework, they might be allowed to listen to the radio a[s] a treat. Very few people had a television set. Sometimes, families would play board games i[n] the evenings as there were no home computers to play games on.

When Mother cleaned the house, she used a broom or a carpet sweeper. Not many people had vacuum cleaners. If she was lucky enough to have a washing machine, it was small and it was filled from the tap with a hose. When the clothes were washed, they were put through a wringer which squeezed out all the water and then they were hung outside on clothes lines. Nearly all clothes had to be ironed in the 50's and the steam iron had not yet been invented. People used dry irons which just used heat. So clothes were sprinkled with water to make them damp and easier to iron.

Understanding

1. Complete these activities using the information report.

    a. Children played hopscotch, _____, _____ or _____ in the street.

    b. Mother filled the washing machine with a _____ from the _____

    c. After doing their homework, children might _____

    or _____.

    d. Sunday dinner was always roast _____ or _____.

. Complete the table comparing the 1950's and the modern day.

The 1950's	The Modern Day
homemade biscuits	microwave snacks
	dishwasher
playing board games	
	vacuum
dry iron	
	air-conditioning
listening to the radio	
	being driven to school
	large, automatic washing machines

Interpreting

. Write full sentences to answer the questions.

a. Why did children play games in the streets? _____

_____

b. Do you think washing the clothes might have taken a long time? Why or why not?

_____

_____

c. How were meals different to modern meals? _____

_____

_____

d. Why were clothes sprinkled with water? _____

_____

Responding

. Write a response to each question in a full sentence.

a. Write two new things you learned about the 1950's.

• _____

• _____

b. When would you prefer to live – the 1950's or now? Give your reasons.

_____

_____

The "Ava" Series

This response was written by Tara Briggs from 3R at Ferny Glen Primary School.

I have been reading a great series of books about a girl named Ava who finds a time machine in an old shed. The time machine takes her to different times in the past and she has amazing adventures in each one. The books have titles like "Ava's Amazing Stone Age Adventure" and "Ava's Amazing Castle Adventure". They are written by Jane Keats.

Ava is a bit shy and quiet at school, but when she is having an adventure, she is brave and can speak up when she needs to. Sometimes, on her travels, she meets people in trouble and can think of good ways to help them. In "Ava's Amazing Stone Age Adventure", she helps a little stone-age girl escape from a hungry Tyrannosaurus Rex. Some of the interesting people in Ava's adventures are King Arthur, Robin Hood and Captain Cook.

Ava usually goes on her adventures on her own which I think is very brave. However, in "Ava's Amazing Pirate Adventure", Ava's big brother, Edwin, follows her to the shed and stows away in the time machine. She doesn't realise he is on board until they land on a pirate ship. Edwin is not good at adventures and Ava has to rescue him from trouble a couple of times. When they return to the present day, Edwin is much nicer to Ava!

The books all have lots of illustrations as well as maps and diagrams that help explain many things to the reader. For example, there is a picture of a huge slingshot in "Ava's Amazing Castle Adventure" to show what weapons were like in the time of knights and castles.

There are fifteen books in the series and so far, I have read five of them. They have all been excellent, but my favourite is "Ava's Amazing Explorer Adventure". This is about Captain Cook's discovery of Australia.

If I had to rate these books, I would give them 5 out of 5! Our school library has them, so get reading!

Understanding

1. Tick the bubble next to information you can find in this text.

a. ◯ The series all has the same main character.

b. ◯ The time machine also travels to the future.

c. ◯ Ava meets a stone-age person.

d. ◯ Tara has read other books by this author.

e. ◯ The books are funny.

f. ◯ Tara's favourite is the one with Captain Cook in it.

g. ◯ Ava fights with a pirate crew.

h. ◯ The books have lots of pictures in them.

i. ◯ Ava's uncle made the time machine.

Choose the correct word in each set of brackets.

a. The review was written by (Tara Briggs / Jane Keats).

b. There are (five / fifteen) books in the series.

c. Ava's brother is called (Edmund / Edwin).

d. Ava's brother is in the (Pirate / Explorer) adventure.

e. The stone-age girl is in danger from a (dinosaur / slingshot).

f. During her adventures Ava is (fearless / scared).

Interpreting

Write a full sentence to answer each question about the text.

a. Tara mentions a number of reasons why she likes the books. What are they?

- _____
- _____
- _____
- _____

b. Write the sentence from the text that suggests Edwin is not always kind to Ava.

_____

c. Write the sentence from the text that tells you Ava has good ideas.

_____

d. Who are some of the people that Ava meets?

_____

e. Write some words or phrases from the text which show you that Ava really likes the books.

_____

f. Where can students easily get the books?

_____

Responding

Answer each question in a full sentence.

a. How do you think the time machine came to be in the old shed?

_____

b. Would you have tried it out? Why or why not?

_____

Don Bradman

Don Bradman, often called 'the boy from Bowral', was born in the NSW town of Cootamundra on 27th August, 1908. He spent his childhood in another country town, Bowral, and this was where he got this name. Don Bradman is known as the greatest batsman and perhaps the greatest cricketer ever.

When Don was a boy, he loved cricket and he spent hours hitting a golf ball with a cricket stump (a straight, thin wooden pole). Don hit the ball against the concrete bottom of a tank stand. When the ball bounced back at him, he tried to hit it again and again. When he was twelve, his father took him to a cricket match at the Sydney Cricket Ground. As he watched the match, Don knew that he wanted to play there one day.

As a teenager, Don began to play for the Bowral team. He was very good and he was soon asked to play for a team in Sydney. Not long after this, when he was nineteen, he was given a place in the NSW team. Then, at twenty years of age, Don was picked to play Test cricket against teams from other countries such as England and India.

Don was a gifted cricketer and often scored centuries (100 runs) so huge crowds watched hi matches. Throughout the 30's, he became famous and wherever he went, people flocked to see him. Don did not really enjoy this!

Don played in 52 Test matches and his average of runs per match was 99.94! No-one has ever matched this. He was often called by another nickname, 'the Don', which showed the respect people had for his talent.

Don retired from cricket in 1948. In 1949, he was made Sir Don Bradman. No other Australian cricketer has been made a 'Sir'. Don Bradman died on 25th February, 2001, at the age of 92. The Prime Minister and many other important people came to his funeral. There are grandstands named in his honour at the Cricket Grounds in Sydney and Adelaide.

Understanding

1. Choose the correct word in each set of brackets.

a. Don Bradman was born in (Bowral / Cootamundra).

b. Don Bradman was a gifted (bowler / batsman).

c. Bradman first played Test cricket when he was (nineteen / twenty).

d. Test cricket is played against other (countries / states).

e. Don Bradman played in (52 / 99) Test matches.

f. Bradman retired from cricket in (1949 / 1948).

Number these events in Don Bradman's life in order from 1 to 6.

a. ☐ Don retires from cricket.   b. ☐ Don is made Sir Don Bradman.

c. ☐ Don is born in Cootamundra.   d. ☐ Don dies at the age of 92.

e. ☐ Don sees a match at the Sydney Cricket Ground.

f. ☐ Don first plays Test cricket for Australia.

Interpreting

Colour the bubble that best fits each question or sentence.

a. In the first paragraph, 'this name' refers to
○ Bowral
○ his birth place
○ a cricketing legend
○ 'the boy from Bowral'

b. The text suggests that as a boy Don
○ had no friends
○ didn't go to school
○ was good at all sports
○ was keen to become a good batsman

c. Don first decided he wanted to play for Australia
○ when he was twelve
○ when he was nineteen
○ when he was playing for NSW
○ when he was playing for Bowral

d. Which word shows that not everyone thinks he was the greatest cricketer?
○ ever
○ known
○ perhaps
○ batsman

e. People called him 'the Don'
○ to make fun of him
○ to show he was famous
○ to show he was the best
○ to show they admired him

f. 'People flocked to see him.' Which sentence has the same meaning as this?
○ A number of people tried to see him.
○ A few people were really keen to see him.
○ Large numbers of people wanted to see him.

g. The text suggests that Don was
○ rich
○ grouchy
○ a bit shy
○ a show-off

Responding

Write a response to each question in a full sentence.

a. Why do you think Don was so good at cricket? Was it talent or lots of practice?

_____

b. Why do you think Don played with a golf ball and a cricket stump?

_____

Terrifying Tales

Contents	
The Mystery of the Giggling Ghost.	6
The Startling Story of Tam, the Cook.	15
The Vampire's Cat.	25
The Foolish Friends	37
The Legend of the Black Lake.	45
The Terrible Tale of Little Freddy.	52
The Adventures of Adam Atkins.	63
The House on the Hill.	71
The Phantom of Beach Street.	85
The Unwelcome Gift.	95
The Goblins' Revenge.	103
The Mystery of the Wizard's Laughter	116

Understanding

1. Complete these activities about the index.

a. Which story comes second last? _____

b. Which story is about an animal? _____

c. Which story is next after "The Adventures of Adam Atkins"?_____

d. Which is the ninth story? _____

e. Which story is about a worker? _____

f. How many stories have people's names in them? _____

g. Which story comes after "The Phantom of Beach Street"? _____

. *Which stories would you find on -*

   a. page 95   _____

   b. page 52   _____

   c. page 37   _____

   d. page 116 _____

   e. page 25   _____

   f. page 63   _____

. *Alliteration is the repetition of beginning words of words, eg. The Giggling Ghost.*

How many stories have alliteration in their titles? _____

Interpreting

. *Colour the bubble which best fits each question or sentence.*

a. Which story is the longest?
- ◯ The Vampire's Cat.
- ◯ The House on the Hill.
- ◯ The Legend of the Black Lake.
- ◯ The Mystery of the Wizard's Laughter.

b. The stories would probably all be
- ◯ fact
- ◯ funny
- ◯ scary
- ◯ recounts

c. How many stories are about mysteries to be solved?
- ◯ one
- ◯ two
- ◯ three
- ◯ four

d. What other word meaning 'ghost' is used in the titles?
- ◯ wizard
- ◯ legend
- ◯ vampire
- ◯ phantom

e. How many stories are about ghosts?
- ◯ one
- ◯ two
- ◯ three
- ◯ four

f. Which story is the shortest?
- ◯ The Foolish Friends.
- ◯ The Unwelcome Gift.
- ◯ The Legend of the Black Lake.
- ◯ The Adventures of Adam Atkins.

g. Which story might be about a haunted house?
- ◯ The House on the Hill.
- ◯ The Phantom of Beach Street.
- ◯ The Goblins' Revenge.
- ◯ The Mystery of the Wizard's Laughter.

Responding

. *Write a response to each question in a full sentence.*

  a. Choose one story and summarise what you think it might be about._____

  _____

  b. Which story would you most like to read? Why? _____

  _____

Ultrasounds are a wonderful part of modern medicine. They are a way of looking inside our bodies without any pain or stress for the patient. They are used often. How do they work?

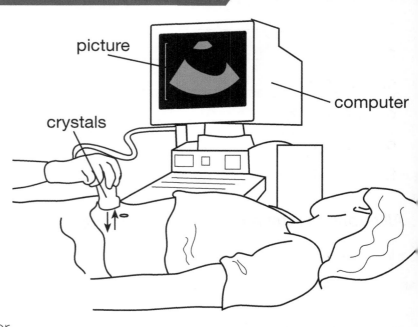

picture

crystals

computer

Ultrasounds use high frequency sound waves and their echoes to build up patterns of places inside our bodies. (High frequency sound waves are ones that are so high we cannot hear them.) The ultrasound has two parts: the computer and the probe. The probe makes the sound waves and sends them into the part of the body the doctor wants to look at. Probes come in different shapes and sizes so they can look at different places in the body.

How does the probe make sound waves? It has special crystals in it. When an electric current is passed through the crystals, they change shape quickly. This change sends sound waves outwards. The probe is passed over the outside of the body. The sound waves travel different distances into the body before they bounce back as echoes. The echoes reach the probe and it sends them on to the computer.

The computer is able to change the echoes into a picture of what is inside the body. This picture can be printed out.

Ultrasounds are a helpful tool for doctors. They can be used to look at organs such as the bladder, liver and kidneys. They can see how blood is flowing around the body. They can allow parents to see a baby before it is born and know whether it is one baby, twins or even triplets!

Understanding

1. Number these steps 1 to 5 in the order they happen in an ultrasound.

a. ☐ The picture is printed.

b. ☐ The probes sends the sound waves into the body.

c. ☐ The computer makes a picture from the echoes.

d. ☐ The echoes bounce back to the probe.

e. ☐ The probe is passed over the body.

Write full sentences to answer the questions.

a. What two parts make up an ultrasound machine? _____

_____

b. What is inside a probe and what do they do? _____

_____

_____

c. Where do the sound waves travel? _____

_____

d. Where do the echoes bounce back to? _____

_____

e. Why don't all probes look the same? _____

_____

f. What are three things ultrasounds can be used for? _____

_____

Interpreting

Colour the bubble which best fits each question or sentence.

a. A good point about ultrasounds is that
- ◯ they are slow
- ◯ they are quick
- ◯ they don't hurt
- ◯ they are cheap

b. 'High frequency sound waves' is an example of
- ◯ extra facts
- ◯ a sentence
- ◯ technical language
- ◯ descriptive language

c. Which word shows the writer's opinion of ultrasounds?
- ◯ tool
- ◯ a way
- ◯ modern
- ◯ wonderful

d. In the third sentence of the third paragraph what does 'they' refer to?
- ◯ the probes
- ◯ the crystals
- ◯ the doctors
- ◯ the sound waves

e. What is the purpose of the diagram?
- ◯ To help in understanding the text.
- ◯ To add more information to the text.
- ◯ To show the different types of probes.
- ◯ To show what an ultrasound machine looks like.

f. What is the purpose of the text?
- ◯ to inform
- ◯ to explain
- ◯ to entertain
- ◯ to persuade

Responding

'High frequency sound waves' is an example of technical language.
Find three more examples of technical language in the text.

- _____
- _____
- _____

My Nan and Pop are wanderers,
They're hardly ever home.
My dad says they've got itchy feet,
Because they really like to roam.

Last Spring, they were in Canada,
Next month, they'll be in Spain,
They loved their time in the south of France,
Next year, they'll go again.

They've seen big ice-bergs, way down south,
And cherry blossoms in Korea,
They've seen New Zealand's bubbling mud,
And lions in Tanzania.

They've trekked in the Himalayas,
They've snorkelled in Fiji,
They've cycled in Vietnam,
They've cruised the wide blue sea.

They've been to India, China, Mexicc
To Hong Kong and Nepal,
They've been to so many countries
They can't remember them all.

I guess they'll keep on travelling,
There's so much still to see,
And they're having such a lot of fun.
I just wish that they'd take me!

Understanding

1. Tick the bubble next to information you can find in this text.

a. ⬭ The grandparents snorkelled in Hawaii.

b. ⬭ They rode bicycles in Vietnam.

c. ⬭ They spent a month in Spain.

d. ⬭ Nan and Pop have probably been to Antarctica.

e. ⬭ They have seen the Pyramids.

f. ⬭ They have been on a sailing ship.

g. ⬭ The grandparents have been on a walking holiday.

h. ⬭ They don't like bus trips.

i. ⬭ Mum and Dad went on one trip with them.

j. ⬭ The grandparents saw tigers in India.

k. ⬭ They usually take two trips a year.

l. ⬭ They went to Canada in Spring.

m. ⬭ They didn't spend very long in Mexico.

n. ⬭ Nan and Pop don't work anymore.

o. ⬭ They saw bubbling mud pools in New Zealand.

Colour the box which contains the correct answer.

a. Where did the grandparents see cherry blossom?

| Japan | Korea | India |

b. To which part of France did they travel?

| north | east | south |

c. What did they see in Tanzania?

| ice-bergs | bubbling mud | wildlife |

d. Where did they do their trekking?

| Spain | the Himalayas | Vietnam |

Interpreting

Colour the bubble which best fits each question or sentence.

a. From the clues in the poem, what do you think 'itchy feet' means?
- ◯ They love to go on treks.
- ◯ They have sore feet now.
- ◯ They like to keep travelling.
- ◯ They can walk long distances.

b. Why can't the grandparents remember all the places they have been?
- ◯ They didn't enjoy all of them.
- ◯ They have been to such a lot.
- ◯ Their memories are getting worse.
- ◯ They have only been to them once.

c. The attitude of the poet to his grandparents is
- ◯ a little jealous
- ◯ upset with them
- ◯ surprised at them
- ◯ worried about them

d. A word with almost the same meaning as 'roam' is
- ◯ walk
- ◯ march
- ◯ wander
- ◯ stagger

e. 'Globe-trotting' means
- ◯ old
- ◯ foolish
- ◯ rushing
- ◯ journeying

Responding

Write a response to each question in a full sentence.

a. Have you been to any of the countries mentioned? Describe your trip.

_____

_____

b. Which of the countries mentioned would you like to visit? Why?_____

_____

Should school hours be longer? Recently, many people have been talking about school hours lasting until 5 or 5.30, instead of ending at 3 or 3.30 as almost all schools do. Is this a good idea? What are the good or bad points of making school hours longer?

If school hours were longer, children would have more time for learning. These days, many subjects are taught in school. If the school day had more hours there would be more time to spend on each one. Students would gain a better understanding of the subject.

On the other hand, students might become very tired if the hours were longer. It is a well-known fact that people cannot learn if they are tired. So longer hours might not be a good idea.

Longer school hours would be helpful to families where both parents work. They would not need to send their children to after-school care. They could just pick them up from school on their way home from work.

However, if school hours were longer, other activities such as sports training or music lessons could not be in the afternoon. They would all have to be in the evening. This would make children even more tired!

There are good and bad points about making school hours longer. After looking at both sides, there seem to be stronger reasons for keeping the hours as they are and not changing them.

Understanding

1. Summarise the reasons for and against having longer school hours.

We should have longer hours.	We shouldn't have longer hours.
_____	_____
_____	_____
_____	_____
_____	_____
_____	_____

Use the words from the box to complete each sentence.

| learn | helpful | subject | parents | working | longer | tired | after-school care |

a. In a _____ school day, students would have more time to spend on each

_____.

b. If children become too _____, they cannot learn.

c. P_____ might not need _____ if school hours were longer.

d. Longer school hours could be _____ to _____ parents.

Interpreting

Write a full sentence for each question about the discussion.

a. How does the writer support his point that people don't learn well if they are tired?

_____

b. How would longer school hours help working parents? _____

_____

c. Why wouldn't having activities in the evening be a good idea? _____

_____

d. Why does the writer decide that school hours should not be longer? _____

_____

Responding

Express your answer in complete sentences.

Do you think school hours should be longer or not? Give two good reasons for your

answer. (Try to find reasons that are not already mentioned.)

_____

_____

_____

_____

_____

Postcard from Wellington

Dear Grandpa,

We are in Wellington now. We came over from Picton this morning on the ferry called the Arahura. It was very rough and Dad said the ferry was rocking and rolling! Once, we hit a big wave and some cups or dishes fell off the shelves and smashed on the floor in the food court. Darcy and I weren't scared, but Harry held Mum's hand all the time.

This afternoon, we visited a museum called Te Papa. It has a giant squid in it and it is massive! I would be scared if I was a diver and I met one under the sea.

Tomorrow, Dad said we will go on a cable-car up to the Gardens and have a picnic there. Darcy likes the trolley buses, too, so we will have a ride somewhere. They're pretty cool.

I'm having a great time. See you next week.

Love,
Cooper

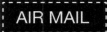

Mr Thomas White

18 Short Street

Wattle Creek

N S W 2222

Australia

Understanding

1. **Tick the bubble next to each sentence with information you can find in this text.**

   a. ⭕ The waves were very big.
   b. ⭕ The waves were three metres high.
   c. ⭕ Four bottles smashed on the floor.
   d. ⭕ The ferry carried cars and trucks.
   e. ⭕ The ferry travelled very fast.
   f. ⭕ The museum is in Wellington.
   g. ⭕ The museum is free.
   h. ⭕ The squid is eight metres long.
   i. ⭕ There are Gardens in Wellington.
   j. ⭕ The cable-car goes to the Gardens.
   k. ⭕ Cooper likes picnics.
   l. ⭕ Cooper will see Grandpa in a week.

2. **Complete these activities about the postcard.**

   a. What was the name of the ferry? _____

   b. What was the name of the museum? _____

   c. What kind of bus will they ride on? _____

   d. Where are they staying now? _____

Colour the bubble that best fits each question or sentence.

a. How many people are in this family?
- ◯ three
- ◯ four
- ◯ five
- ◯ we don't know

b. The postcard is
- ◯ from Grandpa to Cooper
- ◯ from Cooper to Grandpa
- ◯ from Cooper to Mum and Dad
- ◯ from Cooper, Darcy and Harry to Grandpa

c. According to the postcard, what is true of Cooper?
- ◯ The waves were very high.
- ◯ He didn't enjoy the ferry ride.
- ◯ He wants to ride the ferry again.
- ◯ He wasn't frightened on the ferry.

d. Why did Cooper think Harry was scared?
- ◯ Harry said so.
- ◯ Harry held Mum's hand.
- ◯ Harry said he wasn't scared.
- ◯ Harry wanted to get off the boat.

e. Which of these sentences is an opinion expressed by Cooper?
- ◯ 'It was very rough.'
- ◯ 'They're pretty cool.'
- ◯ 'See you next week.'
- ◯ 'Harry held Mum's hand.'

f. What does 'one' in the second paragraph refer to?
- ◯ a diver
- ◯ himself
- ◯ a giant squid
- ◯ the trolley bus

g. We can tell from the postcard that
- ◯ Cooper wants to be a diver.
- ◯ Cooper thinks Harry is a baby.
- ◯ Cooper is enjoying his holiday.
- ◯ Cooper liked the ferry ride best.

h. Dad said the ferry was 'rocking and rolling'. This is an example of
- ◯ facts
- ◯ proof
- ◯ explanation
- ◯ alliteration

Responding

Answer each question in a full sentence.

a. Have you ever been on a rough ferry or boat ride? Tell about it.

_____

_____

_____

b. Why do people send postcards?

_____

_____

Imagine that you could travel anywhere in space.
The timetable might look like this.

Flight	Destination	Departs	Gate
Ace Rockets	Mercury	7.20	7
Starships	Jupiter	7.25	10
Moonrider I	Moon	7.35	11
Mars Express	Mars	7.49	3
Zoom Rockets	Venus	8.05	12
Super Spaceships	Neptune	8.09	17
Outer Planets Rockets I	Saturn	8.25	19
Moonrider II	Moon	8.30	2
Super Shuttle	Mars	8.51	9
Outer Planets Rockets II	Uranus	9.00	18
Marships	Mars	9.06	6
Moonrider III	Moon	9.10	13

Passengers should note that Gates 15 to 20 are at the far end
of the terminal and allow ten minutes' walking time.

Understanding

1. Circle T (true) or F (false) for each sentence.

a. There are three flights to Mars listed.   T   F

b. The first Moon flight leaves 15 minutes before the next one.   T   F

c. There are more than twenty gates.   T   F

d. The flight to Neptune leaves after the one to Jupiter.   T   F

e. Moonrider II leaves at 7.35.   T   F

f. The flight departing at 8.05 goes to Venus.   T   F

g. The Uranus flight is before the Saturn flight.   T   F

h. The Venus flight is the fifth one listed.   T   F

i. The fourth and ninth flights have the same destination.   T   F

j. Starships go to Mars.   T   F

Answer these questions about the timetable.

a. How many flights to the Moon are there? _____

b. How many flights go to Mars? _____

c. How many flights go to Uranus? _____

d. What is the name of the rocket going to Mercury? _____

e. What is the name of the rocket going to Venus? _____

f. What is the name of the rocket going to Neptune? _____

g. Which flight leaves at 8.30? _____

h. Which flight leaves at 9.10? _____

i. What time does Moonrider I to the Moon leave? _____

j. What time does Marships to Mars leave? _____

Interpreting

Colour the bubble that best answers each question.

a. Why might there be so many flights to the Moon and Mars?
   - The fares might be cheap.
   - The flights might be quite short.
   - There could be many people living there.
   - All of the above.

b. Which of these is not listed?
   - Marships
   - Starships
   - Mars Shuttle
   - Zoom Rockets

c. Which of these words does not have a similar meaning to 'zoom'?
   - roam
   - zip
   - whoosh
   - whizz

d. How many different rocket companies fly to Mars?
   - 1
   - 2
   - 3
   - 4

e. What could happen if you don't read the notice at the bottom of the timetable?
   - You will be in trouble.
   - You may miss your flight.
   - The rocket ship won't go on time.
   - Nothing will happen.

Responding

Write a response to each question in a full sentence.

a. Which of these planets would you like to visit and why? _____

_____

_____

b. Do you know why people couldn't really go to some of these places?

_____

The Pied Piper
Part Two

The townspeople were amazed and delighted that the rats had all gone. They clapped and cheered and patted the Piper on the back as he returned to the Town Hall. But, when the Piper asked for the fifty thousand pieces of silver that he had been promised, the Mayor laughed loudly and tried to hand him just fifty pieces of silver. The Piper's face twisted in a snarl.

"But you said you would give me fifty thousand!" he shouted. "You made me a promise! I have taken the rats away as I said I would."

"The rats are gone, never to return," said the Mayor. "Why should we waste fifty thousand pieces of silver? Take your fifty pieces and go!" He turned his back on the Piper.

"You will be sorry for this," promised the Piper and he left. The Mayor laughed to himself, happy that he had saved the town a lot of money and not at all worried about the Piper's threat.

The townspeople slept very well that night because they no longer had to worry about rats running over them or biting them. But, at dawn, the sound of a flute was heard. Only the children heard it and they left their beds and raced out of their houses. The parents slept on peacefully. The children all followed the Piper out of the town, through the forest and up to the foot of a huge mountain. The Piper led them into a great cave and when he played some special notes on his flute, a door closed over the mouth of the cave. One little boy, who had a sore leg and so walked more slowly than the others, arrived just as the door closed. He returned to Hamelin and told everyone what had happened.

There are many different endings for this legend. In some, the children never come back. In other ones, the Pied Piper brings them back when the Mayor pays him fifty thousand pieces of silver.

Understanding

1. Write a full sentence to answer each question about the narrative.

    a. When the Piper asked for his money, what happened? _____

_____

    b. Why did the townspeople sleep well that night? _____

_____

    c. Why didn't they hear the flute at dawn? _____

_____

    d. How did the townspeople find out what had happened? _____

_____

Colour the bubble that best fits each question or sentence.

a. How did the townspeople show their happiness with the Piper?
- ⬭ They laughed loudly.
- ⬭ They patted him on the back.
- ⬭ They were amazed and delighted.
- ⬭ They couldn't believe the rats had gone.

b. The mayor tried to hand him just fifty pieces of silver. 'Tried' suggests
- ⬭ The mayor didn't want to give it to him.
- ⬭ The Piper didn't take it.
- ⬭ It was a fair payment.
- ⬭ The Piper snatched the money.

c. 'In a snarl.' This shows the Piper was
- ⬭ hurt
- ⬭ afraid
- ⬭ angry
- ⬭ surprised

d. From reading the story we know that the Mayor
- ⬭ was sorry
- ⬭ was smart
- ⬭ couldn't be trusted
- ⬭ couldn't be bothered

e. A word with the same meaning as 'great' in 'a great cave' is
- ⬭ grand
- ⬭ famous
- ⬭ wonderful
- ⬭ enormous

f. The Mayor was 'happy' about
- ⬭ sleeping well
- ⬭ the Piper leaving
- ⬭ not paying the Piper
- ⬭ the rats disappearing

g. What is the message of the story?
- ⬭ to keep trying
- ⬭ to keep secrets
- ⬭ to keep your word
- ⬭ to keep to yourself

h. The last paragraph has been added
- ⬭ to finish the story in a good way
- ⬭ to show this is not a factual story
- ⬭ so you can choose your own ending
- ⬭ because the writer didn't know how to finish it

Responding

Write a response to each question in a full sentence.

a. This is not a true story. Find some information in the story which shows this.

_____

b. What do you think of the Mayor? _____

_____

c. What do you think of the Piper's action in this story? _____

_____

d. Write a last paragraph for the story, using the ending you prefer.

_____

_____

_____

_____

Hop-scotch is a game played all over the world. It can be played by girls or boys, alone or in teams. You do not need a ball or any other equipment, just a small stone. You don't need an oval or a court to play on, either. You can just draw a pattern of rectangles on the ground with some chalk and start playing.

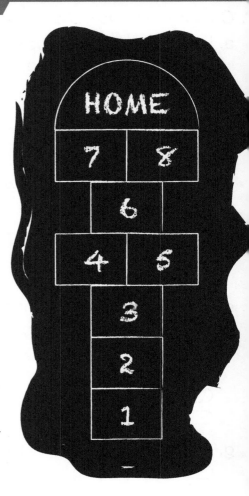

The course for hopscotch is usually made up of a number of squares, with a square, rectangle or semi-circle at the end which is called 'home'. The squares are all numbered in the order they must be hopped. To start the game, a player tosses the stone (marker) into the first square. It must land inside the square and not bounce out. The player then hops through the course, skipping the square with the stone in it. They must only hop and not put down two feet unless there are two squares side by side. When they reach 'home', they turn around and hop back, picking up the marker on the way. The next stage of the game is to toss the marker into the second square and hop through the course again. If a player steps on a line, or loses balance or misses a square, their turn is over. Next time, they start at the same place.

Hop-scotch seems to have been played since the 17th century when it was called 'scotch-hop'. It is played all over the world and has many different names. In India it is called Kith-Kith. In Poland it is called Klasy which means 'classes', while in Italy it is called Campana which means 'little bell'. In France, a course is drawn in a spiral and the game is called Escargot which means 'snail'.

In Australia, we have some different rules for hop-scotch. The marker is called a 'tor', and the game is played in stages. The first stage is hopping. The second stage, called 'jumps', is done by jumping into each square with two feet. The third stage is named 'sizzles' and is the most difficult because the player must jump with legs crossed. The first player to complete all three stages wins.

Understanding

1. Circle T (true) or F (false) for each sentence.

    a. 'Home' is always a semi-circle.   T   F

    b. Hop-scotch is only played by girls.   T   F

    c. Hop-scotch doesn't need special equipment.   T   F

    d. The squares are all numbered in order.   T   F

    e. Hop-scotch is not played in many countries.   T   F

    f. If a player misses a square, their turn is over.   T   F

Circle the correct answer in each set of brackets.

a. In the 17th century, the game was called (hop-scotch / scotch-hop).

b. In Poland, the game is called (Kith-Kith / Klasy).

c. The name 'Campana' in Italy means (little bell / little snail).

d. In Australia, the hardest stage is (jumps / sizzles).

e. You will lose your turn if you (lose balance / lose the marker).

Interpreting

Colour the bubble which best fits each question or sentence.

a. The main idea of the second paragraph is
- ⃝ scoring the game
- ⃝ setting up the game
- ⃝ the procedure of the game
- ⃝ the game around the world

c. The purpose of this text is to
- ⃝ instruct
- ⃝ describe
- ⃝ entertain
- ⃝ persuade

e. Why is there a picture of a hopscotch course?
- ⃝ To help you play the game.
- ⃝ To make the description clearer.
- ⃝ To show another type of course.
- ⃝ The course isn't described in the text.

b. What must the player be sure to do to start their turn?
- ⃝ Not step on a line.
- ⃝ Hop in all the squares.
- ⃝ Not put down two feet.
- ⃝ Toss the marker within the square.

d. Which is not an example of a different name for the game of hopscotch?
- ⃝ tor
- ⃝ Klasy
- ⃝ Kith-Kith
- ⃝ Escargot

Responding

Write a response to each question in a full sentence.

a. Why would hop-scotch be a good game to play in the playground?

_____

b. Why do you think 'sizzles' is the most difficult part of Australian hopscotch?

_____

c. Write two things you learned from reading this text.

- _____

- _____

Leonardo da Vinci

Leonardo da Vinci was one of the most famous artists of all time. He was born on 15th April, 1452 in a little town called Vinci in Italy. His name means 'Leonardo of Vinci'.

Even when he was very small, Leonardo showed that he was very good at drawing. He drew a dragon that looked so real people said they were scared of it! When he was seventeen, he moved to the city of Florence to learn all about painting from a well-known artist. He learned to paint with oil paints which was a new idea.

When he was thirty, Leonardo moved to another city in Italy, called Milan. It was here that he painted 'The Last Supper'. It took him two years to paint it. This is one of the world's greatest paintings. After living in Milan for eighteen years, Leonardo moved back to Florence. It was here that he created his most famous painting, 'The Mona Lisa'. Even though Leonardo had been paid by a rich merchant to paint this, he liked it so much that he kept it! Today, this painting is kept in an art gallery in Paris. Perhaps, one day, you will see it.

Leonardo wanted to be an inventor as well as an artist. He had many ideas for inventions such as tanks, guns, submarines and flying machines. These were not made into real machines while he was alive. However, after he died, some people made models of some of his inventions. This showed that some of the inventions would have worked.

Leonardo lived in France for the last two years of his life. The king had asked him to come there to do some paintings for his palaces. Leonardo spent his time drawing, painting and making notes for new inventions. He died at the age of 67.

Understanding

1. Tick the bubble next to information you can find in this text.

    a. ◯ Leonardo lived with his grandparents when he was small.

    b. ◯ Leonardo liked to scare people when he was a little boy.

    c. ◯ When he was seventeen, Leonardo began to learn about painting.

    d. ◯ Leonardo lived in Vinci till he was seventeen.

    e. ◯ Leonardo liked Milan better than Florence.

    f. ◯ Leonardo took two years to paint 'The Last Supper'.

    g. ◯ Many people said Leonardo's inventions wouldn't work.

    h. ◯ The 'Mona Lisa' is in Paris now.

    i. ◯ Leonardo painted with oil paint.

Number the events of Leonardo's life into the correct order.

a. ☐ Leonardo paints 'The Last Supper'.

b. ☐ Leonardo lives in France for the last two years of his life.

c. ☐ Leonardo learns painting in Florence.

d. ☐ Leonardo moves to Milan.

e. ☐ Leonardo is born in Vinci in 1452.

f. ☐ Leonardo paints the "Mona Lisa'.

Interpreting

Colour the bubble which best answers each question.

a. Which of these statements does the text suggest?
○ Some of his inventions could have been useful.
○ None of his inventions would have worked well.
○ All of Leonardo's inventions would have been useful.
○ All of his inventions should have been made into machines.

b. Which word could best replace 'real' in the fourth paragraph?
○ true
○ good
○ model
○ working

c. What is the main idea of the third paragraph?
○ Leonardo's inventions.
○ Leonardo's good ideas.
○ Leonardo's training as an artist.
○ Leonardo's most famous paintings.

d. 'Perhaps one day you will see it.' Whom is the writer speaking to here?
○ no-one
○ herself
○ Leonardo
○ the reader

e. Why does the writer mention that it took two years to finish 'The Last Supper'?
○ To show how clever Leonardo was.
○ To show that Leonardo painted very slowly.
○ To show what Leonardo was doing at that time.
○ To show how difficult it is to paint a really wonderful picture.

f. Which of these words describes Leonardo best?
○ gifted
○ happy
○ show-off
○ hard-working

Responding

Write a response to each question in a full sentence.

a. Do you think people were really scared of the dragon? Give a reason.

_____

b. What do you think the rich merchant said when Leonardo kept the painting?

_____

cabbage	n. A vegetable with thick green or purple leaves.
cabin	n. 1. A small house. 2. A room on a ship. 3. The area in an aeroplane where passengers sit.
cable	n. A thick rope.
cable car	n. a small cabin hanging from a cable. It is usually used as transport up or down a mountain.
cackle	v. To make a loud cry like a hen.
cactus	n. A prickly plant found in the desert.
caddie	n. A person who carries a golfer's clubs around a golf course.
café	n. A small restaurant selling drinks and light meals.
cage	n. A box made of bars in which an animal or a bird can be kept.
cake	n. A sweet baked food.
calamity	n. a disaster
calcium	n. A mineral that helps bones and teeth grow strong.
calendar	n. A chart of days, weeks and months of the year.
calf	n. 1. The young of some animals such as cows and elephants. 2. The fleshy back part of the leg below the knee.
call	v. To cry out so as to make someone notice you.
calm	adj. Not showing strong feelings such as anger.
camel	n. A large desert animal with either one or two humps on its back.
camellia	n. A shrub with large flowers and shiny leaves.
camera	n. A machine for taking photos or movies.
camp	n. A place where people can stay for a short time, often in tents or in caravans.

Understanding

1. Find the word from the dictionary above.

a. A terrible happening: _ _ _ _ _ _ _ _

b. A flowering plant: _ _ _ _ _ _ _ _

c. Not upset: _ _ _ _

d. A desert animal: _ _ _ _ _

e. A desert plant: _ _ _ _ _ _

f. A vegetable: _ _ _ _ _ _ _

g. A small restaurant: _ _ _ _

h. To make a loud cry: _ _ _ _ _ _ _

i. A small house: _ _ _ _ _

j. A thick rope: _ _ _ _ _

k. A sweet food: _ _ _ _

l. A place for tents: _ _ _ _

Circle the correct word in each set of brackets.

a. The sick tiger was put in a (cabin / cage) for his trip to the zoo's vet.

b. Losing her new phone was a (cackle / calamity) for my sister, Zoe.

c. The (cabin / cable) of the aeroplane became very hot and Grandma felt sick.

d. When Shay fell in the race, he hurt his (cake / calf).

e. The (cactus / camel) is called 'The Ship of the Desert'.

f. It is a good idea to mark important dates on the (camera / calendar).

g. Mum made a delicious salad of (camellia / cabbage).

h. The fees for staying in the (cafe' / camp) were quite low.

Interpreting

Complete these activities.

a. If you were planning a holiday, a _____ would be useful.

b. You would be upset if you lost your _____ while on holidays.

c. When we went on a cruise ship, our _____ was quite large.

d. To get to the top of the mountain, we had to take a _____.

e. My mother's favourite flower is the pink _____.

f. Milk and yoghurt are good for us because they contain _____.

g. The witch gave a loud _____ as she flew off on her broom.

h. Grandpa sometimes hires a _____ when he plays golf.

i. To do well in exams, keep _____ and think carefully.

j. The boat was tied to the wharf with a strong _____.

Responding

Complete this activity and answer the question in a full sentence.

a. What do the letters n., v. and adj. stand for in the dictionary entries?

n. _____, v. _____, adj. _____

b. What are some good reasons for using a dictionary?_____

_____

_____

"This looks interesting," said Mum. She was reading the note that Charlotte had brought home from school. The note was about a community Fun Run to raise money for children in need. The school was asking families in the school to make up teams and enter the run.

"We could do that," Mum went on. "It's a ten kilometre run. It's not until June so we have time to do lots of training."

"I'm not sure I could run that far," said Charlotte.

"You don't have to, Cha Cha," replied Mum. "We'd run as a team, so you could just run some of it."

When Darcy and Levi, Charlotte's twin brothers came home from high school, they thought a family team was a great idea. "Cool! Let's start training, tonight," they suggested. So the five of them, Mum, Dad, Charlotte, Darcy and Levi, as well as Rebel the dog, drove to the local oval. Mum, Dad and Levi ran around it twice and were puffing and red-faced at the end. Charlotte could only do it once and Darcy stayed with her even though he could have run for longer.

The family gave themselves the name, "The Ramsay Rockets" because it sounded catchy. They asked people to sponsor them for every kilometre they ran in the Fun Run. The training was going well and the day of the run was coming closer when disaster struck! Charlotte came home afternoon to find Dad's car in the driveway and Mum sitting in the lounge room with her foot up on a footstool. Her ankle was in plaster.

"Mum fell down some steps at her work and has fractured a bone in her ankle," Dad explained. "She'll need to use crutches for a while."

"No running for me," Mum said, sadly.

But when Darcy and Levi came home from school, they had an idea. "We can push you in a wheelchair!"

That's just what they did. They decorated the wheelchair with streamers and Dad and the twins took turns pushing it. Charlotte sat on Mum's lap when she became too tired to run. The Ramsay Rockets finished the Fun Run and they raised $600 for charity. How good they all felt!

Understanding

1. Answer these questions about the fun run.

a. How long was the run? _____ b. When was it? _____

c. What was the Fun Run for?_____

d. What was the name of the family dog? _____

e. How much did the family raise? _____

Circle T (true) or F (false) for each sentence.

a. Darcy and Leni were twins.   T   F

b. Levi ran around the oval twice.   T   F

c. Mum fell down some steps at home.   T   F

d. Mum broke a bone in her ankle.   T   F

e. They decorated the wheelchair with tinsel.   T   F

f. The team name was 'The Ramsay Rackets.'   T   F

Interpreting

Colour the bubble that best fits each question or sentence.

a. What does Darcy's staying with Charlotte show about him?
- ◯ He gives up easily.
- ◯ He is a caring brother.
- ◯ He is not a very good runner.
- ◯ He doesn't really like running.

b. Why did the twins say 'cool'?
- ◯ They wanted to win the race.
- ◯ They liked the idea of training.
- ◯ They wanted to run as a team.
- ◯ They wanted to push Mum in a wheelchair.

c. At the end of the first night's training Mum, Dad and Levi were
- ◯ tired and hot
- ◯ excited and happy
- ◯ out of breath and hot
- ◯ sore and out of breath

d. Why was Dad's car in the driveway?
- ◯ The car had broken down.
- ◯ It was the day of the Fun Run.
- ◯ He hadn't been working that day.
- ◯ He had come home to look after Mum.

e. A word that has a similar meaning to 'fractured' is
- ◯ bruised
- ◯ pinched
- ◯ cracked
- ◯ knocked

f. 'Children in need' are
- ◯ lost children
- ◯ sick children
- ◯ poor children
- ◯ spoilt children

g. How did the family feel after the Fun Run?
- ◯ tired   ◯ proud   ◯ hungry   ◯ let down

Responding

Write a response to each question in a full sentence.

a. Was the Fun Run a good way to raise money? Give a reason. _____

_____

b. How did the family work as a real team in the Fun Run? _____

_____

Tooth Fairy on Strike!

Monday, July 3rd:

The Tooth Fairy, Prima, has gone on strike! She has been working without stopping for the past two hundred years and in that time, has not had a holiday.

Prima made this statement last night. "Every hour of the day, every day of the week, around the world, some child places a tooth under their pillow and expects that I will take it away and leave money in its place. I am so tired from my job. I just need a break. Surely, another fairy could do my job for a couple of weeks?"

Reports have reached us that Prima has been seen talking to a travel agent. The staff there would not tell exactly where Prima is thinking of going, but they did say she was looking at lots of island holidays.

Children everywhere are shocked at Prima's actions. At Ferny Creek School, some of them spoke to our reporter, Fred Cooke. "I put my tooth under my pillow and in the morning, it was still there!" stated Jeremy. "I don't know what's going on! Last time, she left me some money."

Emily was keen to tell us how upset she was. "I was going to buy stickers with the $2 she usually leaves. I left my tooth, but she didn't leave the money. It's not fair!"

However, Mia had something different to say. "I feel sorry for her. We have holidays. Why can't she have a holiday? We can put our teeth away in a safe place until she comes back, can't we?"

A meeting has been set up on Monday between Prima and the Fairies' Board to see if something can be worked out!

Understanding

1. Write name of the child who made each statement.

a. "I feel sorry for her." _____

b. "It's not fair!" _____

c. "Why can't she have a holiday?" _____

d. "I left my tooth, but she didn't leave any money." _____

e. "I don't know what's going on." _____

f. "I was going to buy stickers..." _____

g. "We can put our teeth away in a safe place..." _____

h. "Last time she left me some money." _____

Match the beginning of each sentence with its correct ending.
There are two more than you need.

| on Monday | at the travel agents | for two hundred years |

| because she needs a holiday | at the shopping centre |

| for weeks and weeks | at Ferny Creek School | on an island |

a. Prima has gone on strike _____.

b. Prima has not had a day off _____.

c. Prima will have a meeting _____.

d. She was seen talking to someone _____.

e. Prima may have a holiday _____.

f. The reporter talked to some children _____.

Interpreting

Write the name of the child who -

a. Cared about Prima _____

b. Wanted to tell how unhappy she was _____

c. Was confused by Prima's actions _____

d. Had different ideas to the other two _____

Responding

Write a response to each question in a full sentence.

a. Was it a good idea for Prima to go on strike? _____

_____

b. What do you think will happen now? _____

_____

c. Think of three good adjectives to describe Prima. _____

_____

d. Prima means 'first'. Why might the Tooth Fairy's name be Prima? _____

_____

Let's Get Fitter

Cooper gave this speech at the weekly Assembly at Ferny Glen School.

Good morning, Mrs Topp, teachers and students,

Our school has become concerned that many of the students are not very fit. They are driven to and from school by their parents or they travel on the school bus. Hardly anyone walks or rides a bicycle to school.

When students are at school, they sit at their desks for at least four and a half hours. When recess and lunchtime comes, do they run about and get some exercise? Hardly anyone does! They sit around again, playing electronic games on their phones. To make matters worse - at the moment, we only have sport on one afternoon for an hour and a half. Students need more than an hour and a half's exercise in a whole week!

Because our school is so concerned that most of the students are becoming more and more unfit, a number of new activities have been planned. The first of these will be the "Walking Bus". Three mornings a week, groups of students will be walked to school by some of our mothers. Each group of ten children will be looked after by two mothers. Do join in! Put your name down with Mr Trapp and he will give you all the information you need.

This year, Year 3 and 4 children can take part in the Cross Country run. They will not have to run as far as the Year 5 and 6 children. There will be training for the Cross Country on Tuesday and Thursday afternoons after school. If you train, you won't find the race so hard, s put your name down with Ms Timms. Another new activity will be twenty minutes of exercise every day before lunch. As well, playing games on your phone at recess and lunch will be banned. Leave your phone in the basket on the teachers' desk. Play handball or soccer instead of electronic games!

All of these changes will help to make us fitter. I am really looking forward to all these new activities!

Understanding

1. Circle T (true) or F (false) for each sentence.

a. Students have sport two afternoons a week.	T	F
b. The "Walking Bus" will be on three mornings a week.	T	F
c. Each group of ten children will have a mother in charge.	T	F
d. Mr Tripp is in charge of Cross Country training.	T	F
e. Exercise will be an everyday activity.	T	F
f. Many children already walk to school.	T	F
g. Phones have to put away in backpacks.	T	F

Draw lines to match each beginning with its correct ending.
There are two more than you need.

a. The Cross Country distance for Years 3 and 4

b. Training for the Cross-country

c. For the 'Walking Bus'

d. For the Cross Country training

e. Daily exercise

will be for twenty minutes before lunch.

will be on two afternoons.

will be the same as for Years 5 and 6.

sign up with Ms Timms.

will not be as long as for the Years 5 and 6.

sign up with Mr Trapp.

sign up with Mrs Topp.

Interpreting

Colour the bubble that best fits each question or sentence.

a. A word that means almost the same as 'concerned' is
   ◯ angry
   ◯ worried
   ◯ thinking
   ◯ confused

b. Why will playing games on phones be banned?
   ◯ It's the rule.
   ◯ Mrs Topp has decided this.
   ◯ So children will talk to their friends.
   ◯ To encourage children to play active games.

c. The aim of the Cross Country training is
   ◯ to help children win
   ◯ to keep the children busy
   ◯ to stop children being bored
   ◯ to improve children's running

d. How does the speaker feel about the exercise program?
   ◯ It's silly.
   ◯ It's a good idea.
   ◯ He doesn't care.
   ◯ Most children will like it.

Responding

Write a response to each question in a full sentence.

a. Why do you think there are two mothers with each group? _____

_____

b. What exercise do you have in your school day? _____

_____

c. How could your school help children be fitter? _____

_____

_____

These bookmarks are easy to make and are lovely gifts.

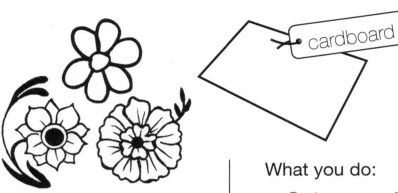

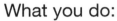

What you need:

• cardboard

• flowers and leaves

• glue

• self-sticking plastic

What you do:

• Gather some flowers and leaves.

• Put the flowers and leaves between two tissues.

• Place the tissues between two sheets of newspaper.

• Put some heavy books on top.

• Leave the flowers and leaves for a few days.

• Cut the cardboard into strips, 4 cm by 14 cm.

• Dab some spots of glue onto the cardboard.

• Arrange the flowers and leaves on the cardboard.

• When everything is dry, cover carefully with plastic.

Understanding

1. Number these steps from 1 to 6, to show the order in which they are done.

Circle all the things you use to make this gift.

Use either 'before' or 'after' to make these statements true.

a. Cut the cardboard into strips _____ you gather the flowers.

b. Put tissues gently around the flowers _____ placing the tissues between sheets of newspaper.

c. The flowers and leaves must be dry _____ you glue them to the cardboard.

d. _____ the glue is dry, cover the strips with plastic.

e. _____ you have made the bookmarks, you can use them as gifts.

Interpreting

Shade the bubble which best fits each question or sentence.

a. The words under 'What you need' are written as
- ⬭ a list
- ⬭ a note
- ⬭ a request
- ⬭ sentences

b. The flowers and leaves are left for a few days
- ⬭ and then stored in a box
- ⬭ so that they are completely dry
- ⬭ so they can be used in other crafts
- ⬭ because you might have other things to do

c. Which of these tells you what to do?
- ⬭ a few days
- ⬭ with plastic
- ⬭ dab some glue
- ⬭ on the cardboard

d. The plastic is used to _____ the bookmarks.
- ⬭ flatten
- ⬭ dry out
- ⬭ protect
- ⬭ gift wrap

e. Putting books on top of the newspaper is the _____ step.
- ⬭ third   ⬭ fourth
- ⬭ fifth   ⬭ sixth

f. The purpose of this text is
- ⬭ to inform   ⬭ to amuse
- ⬭ to instruct   ⬭ to persuade

Responding

Why is using a bookmark a good idea? _____

_____

Trucks carry all kinds of goods from one place to another. The places may be close – from one suburb to another or they may be far apart – from one state to another. Some of the goods the trucks can carry are food, letters and parcels, containers, fuel, milk, concrete and logs.

The big trucks we see on the highways are called semi-trailers. They have two parts, the prime mover and the trailer. The prime mover contains the engine (at least four times more powerful than your family car's engine), the front driving wheels and the driver's cab. Most prime movers have a tiny bedroom behind the cab. On long journeys, the driver pulls into a truck stop at night to sleep. The trailer carries the goods. In some countries, a fully loaded semi-trailer is called a rig.

A road train is a special kind of semi-trailer which has three or four trailers. These road trains travel great distances in the outback of Australia and carry enough fuel so that they do not have to refuel for 3000 km.

Logging trucks are another special type of semi-trailer which carries huge tree trunks cut up at a logging site. The trailer is open and the logs are kept in place by metal rods and cables. The logs are put into the truck by a crane that picks up a pile of logs as if they were a bundle of chopsticks. A logging truck can have two trailers filled with logs. When the logs are emptied out at a saw-mill or loaded onto a ship, the two trailers are folded up so there is just one.

A concrete mixer truck is not a type of semi-trailer, but a very large truck that carries concrete to building sites. About six tons of sand as well as water and cement is loaded into the drum on the back of the truck. As the truck drives, the drum spins around and around, mixing the concrete and stopping it from setting before people are ready for it.

Trucks are very important. Without them, you would not have fresh food in the shops, petrol for the car or parcels from Nanna in the letter-box.

Understanding

1. Tick the bubble next to information you can find in the text.

   a. ⬭ Car carriers can transport ten cars.

   b. ⬭ Some trucks go from one state to another.

   c. ⬭ The prime mover usually has a tiny bedroom.

   d. ⬭ Semi-trailers have air brakes.

   e. ⬭ The goods go in the trailer.

   f. ⬭ About six tons of sand goes into the drum of the concrete mixer.

   g. ⬭ The concrete comes out through a pipe.

   h. ⬭ A concrete mixer is not a semi-trailer.

   i. ⬭ Big dump trucks can be six metres high.

Complete these sentences about trucks.

a. A completely loaded trailer is called a _____ in some countries.

b. Road trains can have _____ or _____ trailers.

c. Road trains can travel _____ km before refuelling.

d. A truck driver may spend the night in a _____ _____.

e. Logging trucks bring logs from the _____ site to the saw-mill or the _____

Interpreting

Colour the bubble that best fits each question or sentence.

a. Why is information put in brackets in the second paragraph?
○ To bring in another idea.
○ To show how large the semi-trailer is.
○ To explain why the truck needs a lot of fuel.
○ To give a better idea of how powerful the engine is.

b. 'As if they were a bundle of chopsticks'. Why does the text make this comparison?
○ To show the size of the logs.
○ To show that the logs are not very heavy.
○ To show that the crane moves very quickly.
○ To show how easily the crane moves the heavy logs.

c. In the last sentence of the fifth paragraph what does 'it' refer to?
○ the truck
○ the drum
○ the concrete
○ the movement

d. The concrete is stopped from setting by
○ the drum
○ the driver
○ the people
○ the movement

e. What is the purpose of the last paragraph?
○ To finish off the report.
○ To show that trucks carry different items.
○ To show how much the writer likes trucks.
○ To encourage the readers to think about how important trucks are in their own lives.

Responding

Answer each question in a complete sentence.

a. How many of the trucks described have you seen? What were they?

_____

_____

b. Write two things from the text that you found interesting. Why did you find them interesting?

_____

_____

Answers

Unit 1: How the Crocodile Got Its Bumpy Skin
1. a. soft and yellow b. muddy c. in the muddy river d. gentle
   e. all day long f. he was better than the other animals
   g. completely changed
2. a. the story is a legend b. pride c. the crocodile's changed
   nature d. the crocodile was punished for his pride
   e. the crocodile is shy about the way he looks now
3. Teacher

Unit 2: Soil
1. a. Sand, clay and silt. b. Top soil, subsoil and bedrock.
   c. top soil d. top soil e. They make burrows and let in air.
2. a. 500 b. cm c. subsoil d. wind e. plants
3. a. very important b. yellow c. aerate d. nutrients e. It will be
   impossible to grow plants. f. Different crops need different
   kinds of soil. g. Plants help to stop soil from blowing away.
4. Teacher

Unit 3: A Dreadful Day
1. a. F b. T c. F d. F e. F f. F g. T h. T i. F
2. a. Charlotte Grey wrote the poem. b. The poet doesn't like
   Corn Pops. c. The poet forgot her hat so she wasn't allowed
   to play. d. 'We walked a long way to school' e. Her mother
   picked her up.
3. a. two b. They arrived at the stop too late.
   c. worse and worse d. finds Maths difficult, but she still
   makes an effort e. better
4. a. The grass stains may have come from falling over while
   playing sport or from sitting on grass. b. Teacher c. Teacher

Unit 4: How to Make Ladybirds
1. a. 2, b. 4, c. 1, d. 5, e. 3
2. a. before b. after c. before d. Before e. after f. after
3. a. a list b. The colours might run if it isn't dry. c. let it dry
   d. fasten e. fifth f. instruct
4. Teacher: Possible answers – It's a quick craft.
   It's easy to get materials.
   b. Teacher: Possible answers – Paperweight, ornament.

Unit 5: Captain Tilly's Treasure Map
1. a. T b. F c. T d. F e. T f. F g. F h. T i. F j. F
2. a. Walk west along Jolly Roger Lane to where it meets
   Rocky Road. Walk north on Rocky Road till it meets Lava
   Lane. Walk west on Lava Lane to Mt Hothead. b. Possible
   answer: Pass through the Happy Hills and walk north towards
   the Shady Swamps. Go around them to avoid crocodiles.
   Continue north, being careful not to go near Mt Hothead in
   case it explodes. c. Mt Hothead is an active volcano so it
   could have a very hot top! d. The map warns about wolves in
   the Wildest Forest of All, the dragon in its den, the crocodiles
   in the Shady Swamps and the quicksand. e. It is about 17 km.
   f. Sail-maker: Pirates often need new sails or old sails to be
   mended. Sword-maker: Pirates need good swords when they
   attack ships. They may need their swords sharpened. Boat-
   builder: A pirate captain may want a new ship or a small boat.
   Baker: Pirates may want bread or cakes to take on a voyage,
   or when they are in port. Pirate Clothes Shop: Pirates need to
   have the right clothes so people will know they are pirates! g.
   Prickle Point h. The villagers fish.
3. a. The treasure is next to the dragon's den – do be careful.
   b. The dragon would scare people away.

Unit 6: Olivia the Princess
1. a. six b. Queen Charlotte c. twenty d. fifty-seven
   e. In the stables. f. Grand-mama / Queen Serena
2. a. disapproving b. She doesn't want to tell him what the book
   is. c. She wants to keep it a secret. d. excited e. all of these
   f. "Olivia's Great Idea." g. a fantasy story
3. Teacher

Unit 7: The Woolly Mammoth
1. a. a, c, e, g, i, j,
2. a. guard hairs b. six tons c. high, domed d. big, sloping
   e. North America f. twenty hours
3. a. The Woolly Mammoth looked something like a modern
   elephant.
   b. humans were the main danger to mammoths.
   d. fearsome-looking e. "Fascinating Prehistoric Animals"
   f. To help us picture the size of the tusks. g. inform
4. Adjectives: tall, giant, terrifying, massive, enormous, furry,
   heavy, hungry

Unit 8: If I Were the Principal
1. a. Teacher
2. a. hours in the classroom b. playing games c. Homework
   d. water games e. a theme park / camping in the bush
3. a. To add more information about the special day. b. exciting
   c. use homework as a punishment d. persuade
4. Teacher

Unit 9: Riley's Diary
1. a. He watched movies on his iPop and played chess with
   Rosie. b. Rosie played with her dolls and played chess with
   Riley. c. They will travel on a moon buggy.
2. a. F b. F c. T d. F e. F f. F g. T h. F i. T j. T k. F
3. a. change into outer clothes b. quite skilled for her age
   c. out of the ordinary d. kind e. to show how take-off felt
4. a,b,c Teacher

Unit 10: What Are Hailstones?
1. a, b, d, f, i
2. a. up, down b. hail c. increases d. heavy
   e. sometimes f. tornadoes
3. a. being lifted b. They hit things with more force.
   c. to encourage the reader to think about the question
   d. terrible e. to help you understand the text
   f. the effects of large hailstones g. technical language
   h. "Wild Weather."
4. Severe thunderstorms, warm air, cold air, thaw, freeze, tornadoes

Unit 11: The Pied Piper – Part One
1. a. T b. T c. T d. F e. T f. F g. F
2. a. The townspeople enjoyed living in the pleasant town of
   Hamelin. b. A large number of rats appeared all of a sudden.
   c. The rats were a danger to people. d. The Piper was tall
   and thin and brightly clothed. e. The Piper asked for one
   thousand pieces of silver. f. The Piper did not pause at the
   river.
3. a. To show that this is a famous legend. b. demanded c. He
   didn't know what he could do. d. to help us picture the scene
   e. a book of legends
4. a. Teacher: Possible adjectives – relieved, delighted,
   surprised, shocked. b. Teacher

Unit 12: Life in the 1950's
1. a. football, skipping and chasing games b. hose, tap
   c. listen to the radio, play board games d. chicken, lamb
2. a.

The 1950's	The Modern Day
homemade biscuits	microwave snacks
washing dishes by hand	dishwasher
playing board games	playing on the computer
carpet sweeper	vacuum
dry iron	steam iron
coal or wood burning fire	air-conditioning
listening to the radio	watching television
walking or riding a bike	being driven to school
no washing machine or small washing machine with a wringer	large, automatic washing machines

3. a. There was not as much traffic so streets were safer. b.
   Yes, because the washing machine had to be filled with a
   hose, the clothes put through a wringer and the clothes were
   hung outside. c. Food was simpler – meat with vegetables or
   a stew. Everyone ate together. Sunday dinner was the most
   important meal of the day and was a roast. d. The water
   made them damp and easier to iron.
4. Teacher

Unit 13: The "Ava" Series
1. a, c, d, f, h
2. a. Tara Briggs b. fifteen c. Edwin d. Pirate e. dinosaur
   f. fearless
3. a. Reasons can be: great adventures, lots of interesting
   information, illustrations and diagrams. b. When they return to
   the present day, Edwin is much nicer to Ava. c. Sometimes
   on her travels, she meets people in trouble and can think of
   good ways to help them. d. Robin Hood, King Arthur and
   Captain Cook are some of the people she meets.
   e. Some of the words and phrases Tara uses are: great,
   amazing adventures and 5 out of 5. f. The books are

available in the school library.
Teacher

Unit 14: Don Bradman
a. Cootamundra b. batsman c. twenty d. countries e. 52
f. 1948
c, e, f, a, b, d
a. 'the boy from Bowral' b. was keen to become a good
batsman c. when he was twelve d. perhaps e. to show they
admired him f. Large numbers of people wanted to see him.
g. a bit shy
Teacher

Unit 15: Terrifying Tales
a. The Goblins' Revenge b. The Vampire's Cat c. The House
on the Hill d. The Phantom of Beach Street e. The Startling
Story of Tam the Cook. f. 3 g. The Unwelcome Gift
a. The Unwelcome Gift b. The Terrible Tale of Little Freddy
c. The Foolish Friends d. The Mystery of the Wizard's Laughter
e. The Vampire's Cat f. The Adventures of Adam Atkins
6
a. The House on the Hill. b. scary c. two d. phantom e. two
f. The Legend of the Black Lake g. The House on the Hill

Unit 16: How Does An Ultrasound Work?
e,b,d,c,a
a. The two parts are the probe and the computer.
b. There are crystals inside the probe which change shape
when an electrical current is passed through them. This
change sends out sound waves. c. The sound waves travel
different distances into the body. d. The echoes travel back to
the probe. e. Probes come in different shapes and sizes. f.
Ultrasounds can look at organs in the body, at how blood flows
and at unborn babies.
a. they don't hurt b. technical language c. wonderful d. the
crystals e. to help in understanding the text f. to explain
Computer, probe, sound waves, crystals,
electric current, echoes.

Unit 17: Globe-trotting Grandparents
b, d, g ,l ,o
a. Korea b. south c. wildlife d. the Himalayas
a. They like to keep travelling. b. They have been to such a lot.
c. a little jealous d. wander e. journeying
Teacher

Unit 18: Should School Hours Be Longer?
a. Teacher
a. longer, subject b. tired c. Parents, after-school care
d. helpful, working
a. The writer says 'it is a well-known fact'. b. They would not
need after-school care but could pick up their children straight
from school. c. The children would become even more tired.
d. The writer looks at both sides and decides the arguments
for keeping the hours the same are stronger.
Teacher

Unit 19: Postcard from Wellington
a, f, i, j, l
a. Arahura b. Te Papa c. a trolley bus d. in Wellington
a. five b. from Cooper to Grandpa c. He wasn't frightened on
the ferry. d. Harry held Mum's hand. e. 'They're pretty cool.'
f. a giant squid g. Cooper is enjoying his holiday. h. alliteration
a. Teacher b. Postcards are sent to family and friends to tell
what you are doing on your holiday.

Unit 20: Blast Off!
a. T b. F c. F d. T e. F f. T g. F h. T i. T j. F
a. three b. three c. one d. Ace Rockets e. Zoom Rockets
f. Super Spaceships g. Moonrider II to the Moon
h. Moonrider III to the Moon. i. 7.35 j. 9.06
a. All of the above b. Mars Shuttle c. roam d. 3
e. You will miss your flight.

Unit 21: The Pied Piper – Part Two
a. The Mayor tried to give him fifty not fifty thousand pieces of
silver. b. The piper didn't take it.. c. Only the children heard
the flute. d. A little boy who was left behind told them.
a. They patted him on the back. b. tried c. angry d. couldn't
be trusted e. enormous f. not paying the Piper g. to keep
your word h. to show this is not a factual story
Teacher (For a. all the magic elements.)

Unit 22: Hopscotch
a. F b. F c. T d. T e. F f. T g. T
a. Scotch-hop b. Klasy c. little bell d. sizzles e. lose balance
a. the procedure of the game b. Toss the marker within the

square. c. describe d. tor e. To make the description clearer.
4. a,b,c Teacher

Unit 23: Leonardo da Vinci
1. c, d, f, h, i
2. e, c, d, a, f, b
3. a. Some of his inventions could have been useful. b. working
   c. Leonardo's most famous paintings. d. The reader.
   e. To show how difficult it is to paint a really wonderful picture.
   f. gifted.
4. a, b Teacher

Unit 24: Look It Up.
1. a. calamity b. camellia c. calm d. camel e. cactus
   f. cabbage g. café h. cackle i. cabin j. cable k. cake l. camp
2. a. cabin b. calamity c. cabin d. calf e. camel f. calendar
   g. cabbage h. camp
3. a. calendar b. camera c. cabin d. cable car e. camellia
   f. calcium g. cackle h. caddie i. calm j. cable
4. a. noun, verb, adjective b. Teacher

Unit 25: The Fun Run
1. a. 10 km b. June c. To raise money for children in need.
   d. Rebel e. $600
2. a. F b. T c. F d.T e. F f. F
3. a. He is a caring brother. b. They wanted to run as a team.
   c. out of breath and hot d. He had come home to look after
   Mum. e. broken f. poor children g. proud
4. It was fun to do so people would want to either join in
   or support it.

Unit 26: Tooth Fairy on Strike
1. a. Mia b. Emily c. Mia d. Emily e. Jeremy f. Emily
   g. Mia h. Jeremy
2. a. Prima has gone on strike because she needs a holiday.
   b. Prima has not had a day off for two hundred years.
   c. Prima will have a meeting on Monday. d. She was seen
   talking to someone at the travel agents. e. Prima may have
   a holiday on an island. f. The reporter talked to some children
   at Ferny Creek School.
3. a. Mia b. Emily c. Jeremy d. Mia
4. Teacher

Unit 27: Let's Get Fitter
1. a. F b. T c. F d. F e. T f. T g. F
2. a. The Cross Country distance for the Years 3 and 4 will not
   be as long as for the Years 5 and 6. b. Training for the Cross
   Country will be on two afternoons. c. For the "Walking Bus"
   sign up with Mr Trapp. d. For the Cross Country Training sign
   up with Ms Timms. e. Daily exercise will be for twenty minutes
   before lunch.
3. a. worried b. to encourage children to play active games
   c. to improve children's running d. It's a good idea.
4. a. Possible reasons: safety, children getting to school
   on time. b,c, Teacher.

Unit 28: A Simple Gift
1.
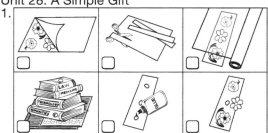
2. Items needed are: scissors, ruler, pencil, flowers, glue,
   cardboard, roll of plastic
3. a. after b. before c. before d. After e. After
4. a. a list b. so that they are completely dry c. dab some glue
   d. protect e. fourth f. instruct
5. Teacher: Possible reasons – You won't lose your place. /
   You won't damage the book by turning down the page.

Unit 29: Trucks
1. b, c, e, f, h
2. a. a rig b. three / four c. 3000 d. truck stop
   e. logging, ship
3. a. To give a better idea of how powerful the engine is.
   b. To show how easily the crane moves the logs. c. the
   concrete d. the movement e. To encourage readers to think
   about how important trucks are in their own lives.
4. a,b,c Teacher

Reading Skills Record

Evaluation and assessment are an important part of any reading and comprehension program. Assessment by the teacher, parent or even the child is an important part of this program. Completing the Reading Skills Record assists in the monitoring of reading skills as the year progresses. A simple tick, term by term, when the identified skill has continued to be achieved.

SKILLS	Term 1	Term 2	Term 3	Term 4
Reads silently.				
Reads and interprets a variety of text types.				
Shows interest in and understands narratives and poems.				
Shows interest in and understands information reports, descriptions, recounts, discussions and expositions.				
Understands and interprets non-text material such as maps and timetables.				
Recognises the main characters in a narrative.				
Recognises the setting in a narrative.				
Can distinguish fantasy from reality.				
Can distinguish fiction from non-fiction.				
Follows instructions.				
Scans text to locate specific information.				
Uses contextual clues to find answers to questions.				
Uses inferential clues to discover meaning.				
Identifies main ideas.				
Identifies logical sequence.				
Chooses right answers from a number of alternatives.				
Decides on the correctness of statements.				
Composes written answers to questions.				
Relates text to personal experience.				
Makes decisions on the basis of given information				
Makes predictions using given information.				
Demonstrates a widening vocabulary.				